Warrior Princess

Ignite Your Inner Warrior

An Eight-Week Study

Shelley Wilburn

Warrior Princess

Ignite Your Inner Warrior

An Eight-Week Study

A powerful Bible study that will resonate with every woman and compel them to rise up, to unshackle whatever chains bind them, and to become a true *Warrior Princess* in God's army.

— *Dora Hiers, Author of Heart Racing, God-Gracing Romance and Amazon Bestselling Author of the Harmon Heritage series*

Warrior Princess: Ignite Your Inner Warrior is a call to action. This interactive Bible study is more than a guide, it's a foundation for your personalized journey to grow up and grow strong as a woman of faith.

-*Lisa Lickel, Author of What If stories with a twist of grace*

One of the foundational principles in life is to understand who you are. If you can understand who you are, then you'll know what you can do and are purposed to do in life. In this book, Shelley Wilburn lays out very clearly how you can find out who you are, thereby understanding what you have been purposed to do in life. Life is much simpler, and more enjoyable, when the questions surrounding you are answered. This book will help you along life's way.

-*Jason McKinnies, Senior Pastor, Southern Illinois Worship Center, Herrin, Illinois*

Warrior Princess is a fantastic book study to follow Walking Healed. It's important to know you are a warrior in the army of God. Raise your sword! It's time to walk, talk, and fight for the Kingdom of God.

-*Lanna Ewell, Herrin, Illinois*

Warrior Princess is a Bible study to aid in discovering your true identity in Christ. When you know your identity, you have a better understanding of God's plan and purpose in your life.

-*Brenda West, West Frankfort, Illinois*

Warrior Princess
Copyright © 2018 Shelley Wilburn

Photographs by Alanna Milby Photography
Cover Design by Rodney Schroeter
Coloring Page Illustrations by Shelley Wilburn
Edited by Lisa J Lickel

Spirituality
ISBN 978-0-9864311-3-5

Library of Congress control number: 2018905759

All rights reserved. No part of this publication may be reproduced, stored in a retrieval system, or transmitted in any form or by any means, electronic, mechanical, photocopying, recording, or otherwise without the prior written permission of the author. Reviewers may quote briefly for review purposes.

Quote from the song "Come Alive" (Dry Bones), Copyright © 2014 CentricSongs (SESAC) "See You At The Pub" (SESAC) (adm. At CapitolCMGPublishing.com) / Warner Chappell Music (ASCAP) All rights reserved. Used by permission.

Scripture quotations are taken from the Holy Bible, New Living Translation (NLT), copyright ©1996. Used by permission of Tyndale House Publishers, Inc. Carol Stream, IL USA. All rights reserved.

Scripture quotations are taken from the Amplified Bible, Old Testament. Copyright © 1965, 1987 by the Zondervan Corporation. Used by permission. All rights reserved.

Scripture quotations are taken from the Amplified Bible, New Testament. Copyright © 1954, 1958, 1987 by the Lockman Foundation. Used by permission.

Scripture quotations marked "NKJV" are taken from the New King James version. Copyright © 1982, Used by Thomas Nelson, Inc. Used by permission. All rights reserved.

Scripture taken from THE MESSAGE. Copyright © 1993, 1994, 1995, 1996, 2000, 2001, 2002. Used by permission of NavPress Publishing Group.

Scripture taken from The Expanded Bible (EXB). Copyright ©2011 by Thomas Nelson. Used by permission. All rights reserved.

Scripture taken from the New Century Version®. Copyright © 2005 by Thomas Nelson. Used by permission. All rights reserved.

Scripture quotations are from the ESV® Bible (The Holy Bible, English Standard Version®), copyright © 2001 by Crossway, a publishing ministry of Good News Publishers. Used by permission. All rights reserved.

Scripture taken from the NEW AMERICAN STANDARD BIBLE®, Copyright ©1960,1962,1963,1968,1971,1972,1973,1975,1977,1995 by The Lockman Foundation. Used by permission.

All glossary definitions taken from Merriam-Webster Online Dictionary copyright ©2015 by Merriam-Webster, Incorporated

Warrior Princess

Table of Contents

- Dedication i
- Note from the Author ii
- Introduction iv
- Week One 1
  - Valley of Dry Bones
  - Valley of Dry Bones Coloring Page 8
  - Valley of Dry Bones Journal Page 9
- Week Two 10
  - Battle Lines
  - Battle Lines Coloring Page 19
  - Battle Lines Journal Page 20
- Week Three 21
  - Basic Training
  - Basic Training Coloring Page 30
  - Basic Training Journal Page 31
- Week Four 32
  - Your Assignment
  - Your Assignment Coloring Page 40
  - Your Assignment Journal Page 41
- Week Five 42
  - Prepare for Battle
  - Prepare for Battle Coloring Page 51
  - Prepare for Battle Journal Page 52
- Week Six 53
  - Worship is Warfare
  - Worship is Warfare Coloring Page 66
  - Worship is Warfare Journal Page 67
- Week Seven 68
  - Arise, Warrior Princess!
  - Arise, Warrior Princess Coloring Page 80
  - Arise, Warrior Princess Journal Page 81
- Week Eight 82
  - Live Free, Live Brave
  - Live Free, Live Brave Coloring Page 91
  - Live Free, Live Brave Journal Page 92
- Who I am in Christ 93
- Debriefing 94
- What Do All Those Links Mean? 96
- What Does A Warrior Princess Look Like? 97
- Appendix A 98
  - How to Accept Jesus into Your Heart
- Glossary of Armor 100
- Endnotes 101
- Other Books by Shelley Wilburn 104
- About the Author 105

Dedication

I dedicate this book to my favorite Warrior Princesses; my two, beautiful daughters, Rachel and Katie, and to my beautiful daughter-in-love (and cover model), Rhiannon. You, my dear daughters, are more than you know, and God is much more than you know! I am so proud of the women you have become. You inspire me, every day, to be more: a better wife, a better mom, a better mother-in-law, and a better Nonney. I also dedicate this book to Warrior Princesses everywhere, of every age, of every race. We are women. We are sisters in Christ. We are Warrior Princesses. There is nothing to separate us, dear sisters. To everyone who has ever struggled, or felt less than, this book is for you. If you ever embrace who you truly are, you will be a force to be reckoned with. This book was written to help you do that. Stand tall, dear warriors. Embrace your true identity. Step out into your calling. The God of the universe is crazy about you, and you are magnificent!

Note from the Author

Instructions for What to Expect Through This Study

This book has been over four years in the making. It started with me trying to write a devotional using various words I had taken from the Bible to discover where I fit in. I had no idea at the time that it was not about where I fit in. I got halfway through the devotional and it was going nowhere so I set it aside thinking, one day I'll finish that. Yet, it bugged me to leave a book unfinished.

Not long after, I was driving to the train station at two o'clock in the morning to pick up my daughter and grandson when I was suddenly inspired with a flood of information. Because I was driving, I whipped out my phone and managed to find the voice recorder and just started talking into it, recording the notes. I once heard a pastor of mine say, "*God is a God of suddenlies*." This was my *suddenly*. God gives great notes in the middle of the night! These were the beginnings of Warrior Princess. I even had the title. However, I had yet to connect the dots between these notes and my notes in the devotional folder. It would be another year or so before those dots connected, including the writing of two other books. I also had to discover my own identity in Christ.

Now here we are, together, ready to take the journey. Take a few moments and familiarize yourself with this book. We begin here in the introduction. We will move through each chapter together, discovering some interesting and exciting truths about who God says we are. Throughout the study you will discover hints to *your* true identity in Christ. I have called these hints ***links***; words that describe things about you and I that we find in God's Word. They will be in italics and bold so you can reference them later throughout the book. As you discover them, write them in the back of the book titled, **Who I Am in Christ**. When you finish this study, you will have a wonderful list of words describing from God's Word, who He says you are. You can then dub yourself His *Warrior Princess*.

At the end of each chapter there are two special pages – a coloring page with a Scripture from that chapter and a journal page for you to write special things that have inspired you in that particular chapter such as a prayer, idea, or Scripture passages that you may want to remember for further study (it is also a coloring page).

As I wrote this book, I allowed the Holy Spirit to guide me in the passages He wanted me to highlight. However, a remarkable thing was happening and I only noticed it as I came closer to finishing the study. Nearly every long passage referred to the LORD in all capital letters. This is monumental. It means something and I wanted to share it with you here before we get started because I want you to be on the lookout for it as well.

While doing a Bible study by Beth Moore*, I learned that in the formal versions of the Bible, as opposed to most modern paraphrases, when you see references to ***Lord***, this is the Hebrew transliteration and is a form of ***Adonai***, emphasizing God's lordship and His position as Master. When you see references to ***LORD*** (in all caps), the Hebrew transliteration is ***YHWH*** and emphasizes His position as covenant maker and keeper. When you see references to ***God***, the Hebrew transliteration is ***Elohim*** and emphasizes His position as universal Creator.

What a rich blessing to learn the meanings of His name just how they are projected or spelled out in Scripture! I feel so blessed by this revelation. I want you to be blessed as well. Therefore, bookmark this page and throughout this study, whenever you see any reference to the Lord, regardless of spelling, circle it and refer back to this description to get a deeper meaning of the passage and what He is saying to you. I'll remind you periodically: Lord, Adonai; LORD, YHWY, covenant maker and keeper; God, Elohim, universal Creator.

I also want to make note that I used various translations of the Bible throughout this study. This is important because they each bring out a deeper meaning to that particular passage. I have listed the translation after each passage. Also, to avoid having footnotes at the bottom of the page and to prevent disrupting the reading with endless references, you will also find a complete listing of Scripture and their translations in the Endnotes section at the back of the book.

As you read through this study, let the Holy Spirit speak to you. And as you learn, write your answers on the lines given, but also get bold and write notes in the margin of your workbook. Use it as a guide, a treasure map if you will, to discover your true identity and the One who calls you by that name.

Introduction

There is a battle going on. It has been going on since before time began. God was fully aware of it, but He chose to move forward with His plan. Why? Because, God's plan is infallible. It's perfect. Yet, while there has been seemingly one disaster after another, each one has worked perfectly into His plan…including the creation of *you*.

Dear sisters in Christ, lovely, beautiful ones, you are part of God's wonderful, amazing, larger-than-life plan. That is exciting! But we need to address some things before we can begin to move into the position He has created for each of us.

Many of you don't know your part in this great plan. Even more of you have no idea who you really are in Christ. You just don't know your true identity. How then can you operate in the gifts and the calling God has on your life?

Maybe you're wondering, *There's a calling on my life? How can that be? God couldn't possibly use me!* Oh, precious one, there *is* a call on your life and God absolutely *can* use you. Through the pages of this study we are going to take a journey to uncover your true identity. By the time we finish, you will be equipped to take your place as God's own Warrior Princess.

It may sound ridiculous to you right now. It's not.

We *are* who God says we are. He says a lot about us and that is our identity. He says we are more than conquerors (Romans 8:37). That means we are victorious in everything and then some. We exceed, or go beyond that victory. Why? Because when Jesus defeated Satan once for all, He did more than just win the battle over death. Jesus got up from the grave. He beat hell so we wouldn't have to go there, eternally separated from Him. He did all that so we wouldn't have to suffer. He conquered it all, took back the keys to death, hell, the grave, the kingdom, everything—He did it for you. He did it for me.

Being saved is so much more than a ticket to heaven. There is so much more and too many are missing out on their *more* because they stop at salvation. Honey, you are more than a victor. You go beyond that into the realm of royalty, to having the power to tell the devil to take a hike.

> For an example of how our prayers are prevented from being answered, read Daniel 10:12-14

You need to know the devil wants to mess you up. He will stop at nothing to make things miserable for you, including hindering your prayers. There are times when there are spiritual wars going on above you, in the heavenlies, that prevent your prayers from being answered. However, you have the spiritual power, and authority over him, and he hates you for it.

There are many who are discovering that daily. They are learning their true identity and stepping into their role as Warrior Princesses and, because of that, there's an army rising up. They have stepped over the battle lines. It's time to put on our full armor and prepare to run, full-on, at the enemy, sword raised, battle cry on our lips.

We *will* be victorious, make no mistake. We will not be defeated. There will be no casualties of this war. No. No casualties. For this war is already won. All we have to do is stand, then watch the Lord fight for us. And He *will* fight for us.

Don't misunderstand, if we do nothing, this battle won't be fought. We, as women, as Christ followers, as Warrior Princesses, must rise and stand our ground in order to be victorious.

Our identity is at stake here. Our enemy is trying to steal the very essence of who we are as women. He's using many different areas and people to do it, too. It's up to us to put our foot on his neck and take back what is rightfully ours. It *can* be done. It *must* be done. Are you ready?

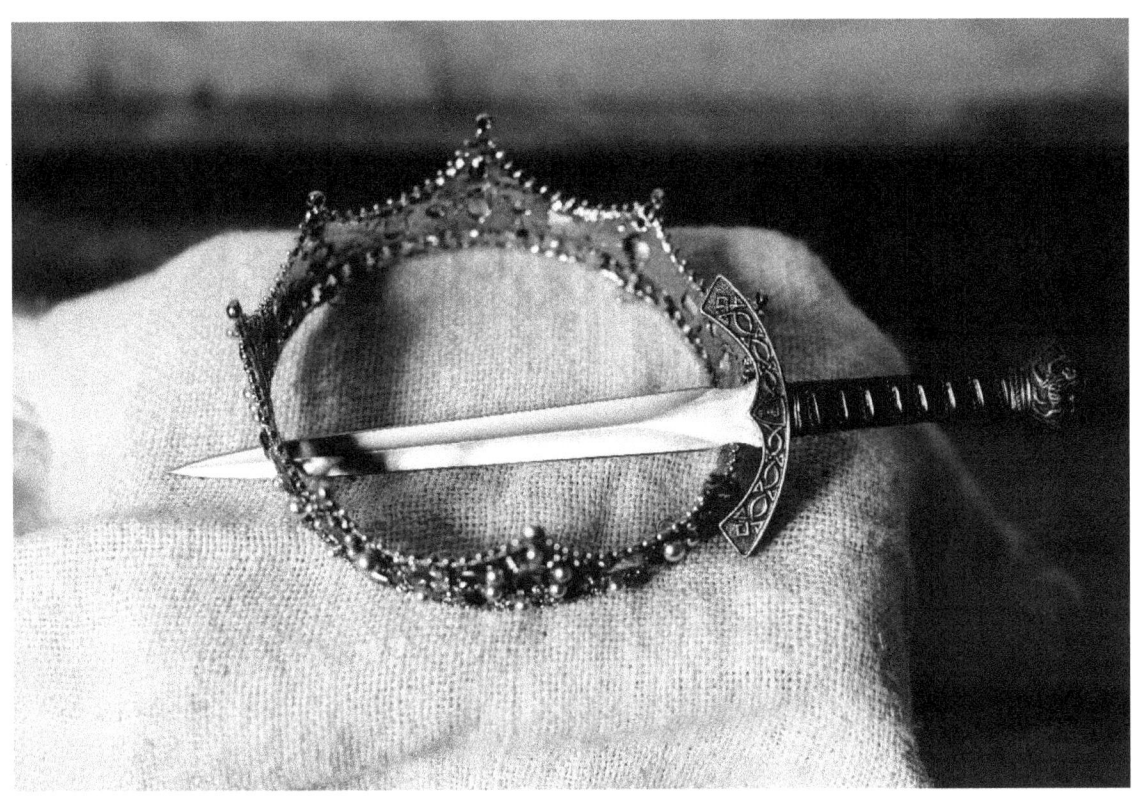

Week One

Valley of Dry Bones

Bringing the Dead Back to Life

Up out of the ashes let us see an army rise. We call out to dry bones, come alive!
 - "Come Alive" (Dry Bones), by Lauren Daigle, How Can This Be, Deluxe Edition

What if I told you that you were more than you know? What if I were to tell you that you were actually royalty, a princess? Would you believe me? Would you laugh, snicker, roll your eyes? What if I told you that not only are you royalty but you're a warrior as well?

You may not feel like a warrior right now, much less a princess. I can totally understand and identify with your feelings. I have been there myself. Maybe you're thinking or even saying, "How can I be a warrior? Everyone intimidates me. I never stand my ground. I always back down, or give in. How can I possibly be a warrior? So forget about me being a Warrior Princess." I get that.

Oh, lovely ones, God has something to say to you. In fact, He has a lot to say to you. And with that, we are going to move into discovering your true identity because you have a Prince pursuing you. You have a King Who loves you crazy, madly, deeply. Sounds like a fairytale, doesn't it? It's not. It's for real, He is for real, and your true identity is for real.

You have been led to believe you're just dried up, useless, worth nothing to God. But it's all a lie and it comes straight from the enemy of your soul. You, dear ones, *are* each a Warrior Princess.

First, though, we have to really know who we are in Christ. Walk down any street, store aisle, parking lot, home, school, anywhere and you will see dry bones; women who merely exist but don't really live. Why is that? Some look happy. Some act happy. Their clothes, shoes, cars, even their homes all dictate happy, healthy, thriving human beings. True. Physically, they are.

However, look deep inside each one of them and even ask them pointedly if they are happy and they will tell you a completely different story.

I wish I was thinner.
I wish I was prettier.
I just wish people would see me.
No one knows the pain I suffer.
I deal with depression.
I'm so afraid.
I deal with anxiety.
I'm not worth anything.
I'm not smart.
I'm so alone.
I have no one.
No one cares about me.

On, and on, and on these statements could go and would probably describe many people you know, or maybe even yourself. Some may even lie and tell you that they are perfectly happy and their lives are perfect. Yet, inside they live in shame and guilt, not wanting anyone to know the truth because to them it would be devastating.

It can happen to anyone, even Christians. This is how the enemy tricks us into believing that we aren't good enough and especially not good enough for God. Believing the lies of the enemy, we wither and withdraw into ourselves, thereby becoming nearly lifeless inside, merely existing. That's how the enemy prevents us from living the abundant life God wants us to have.

We live in a valley of dry bones and don't even know it. But God has other plans for those bones. He wants them to live and breathe again. He wants *you* to live and breathe again. Can dry bones live again? Let's find out.

In the book of Ezekiel, the LORD took Ezekiel in the Spirit and showed him a valley filled with dry human bones. These bones were actual dried up, dead bones; lifeless, without skin, blood, or breath. Yet, God had a plan and showed Ezekiel something profound.

Read Ezekiel 37:1-14 (I used the New Living Translation, or NLT) then answer the questions below.

What was the first thing the LORD asked Ezekiel? _____

What was Ezekiel's answer? _____

Do you think Ezekiel believed that God could make the bones living people again? Why or why not?
_____

Read verse 6 of that passage again. What prophetic message did the LORD tell Ezekiel to speak to the bones? _____
_____

In the New Testament, just after Jesus rose from the dead, He appeared to His Disciples. They had been hiding in a locked room, afraid of the Jewish leaders. However, Jesus was suddenly before them, proving He had risen just as He had promised.

After showing them His wounds they were all filled with joy. Then Jesus encouraged them by saying, "Peace be with you. As the Father has sent Me, so I am sending you" (John 20:21 NLT).

In keeping with the theme of Ezekiel 37, read John 20:22. What did Jesus do next?
_____

What happened after He breathed on them? _____

Now look back at Ezekiel 37:5-6. What did the Sovereign LORD say? _____
_____

Compare the two verses. What similarities do you see? _____
_____

Jesus breathed on the disciples and they received the Holy Spirit. They became truly alive. In Ezekiel's story, the LORD told him to speak a prophetic message to the bones and say to them that the Sovereign LORD said He was going to put *breath* into them and make them live again.

When you read Ezekiel's account, you see the bones begin to rattle together and stand. They were put back together and they did live again. But let's read and see what else God said about the bones.

Read Ezekiel 37:11.

What did the LORD say the bones represented? _____

According to the LORD, what were the bones saying? _____

_____

They had lost all hope. But look in verse 14. What did the LORD say He was going to put into them? What were they going to do? _____

God has great plans for each of us. He wants to breathe life back into us through His Spirit, the Holy Spirit, so we can live again and return home someday. Our heavenly home.

Through the circumstances of our lives, though, we shrivel and waste away until we resemble those dry bones in the valley. Or, like the disciples, we lock ourselves away in fear.

The enemy tries to wear us down and make us believe that we are no longer useful to God or anyone. However, Jesus debunks every attack of the enemy. ***Read below.***

> God has great plans for each of us.

"The thief comes only in order to steal and kill and destroy. I came that they may have and enjoy life, and have it in abundance (to the full, till it overflows)." ~John 10:10 (Amplified Bible)

What does the enemy come to do?
_____

What are some areas of your life the enemy is trying to steal, kill or destroy? List them below. I've given you a few to help jumpstart you.

<u>Peace, faith, joy,</u>_____

_____

_____

*What did Jesus say **He** came for?* _____

_____

We often feel as if we are being tempted and attacked in every direction. Jesus knows what we're going through, because He lived it all too. He understands and He cares.

Read Hebrews 4:14-15 (NLT) below, then answer the questions.

"So then, since we have a great High Priest who has entered heaven, Jesus the Son of God, let us hold firmly to what we believe. This High Priest of ours understands our weaknesses, for he faced all of the same testings we do, yet he did not sin."

What does it say Jesus faced? _____

Jesus has faced everything we have faced but with one difference. What is it? _____

_____

Have you noticed the spelling of the LORD'S name in Ezekiel? Remember, the Hebrew transliteration is YHWH (Yahweh) and emphasizes His position as covenant maker and keeper. Read back through and note that He was, in fact, making a covenant with Ezekiel.

Now let's back up a couple of verses in Hebrews and clear something up.

Read Hebrews 4:12-13 (NLT) below.

"For the word of God is alive and powerful. It is sharper than the sharpest two-edged sword, cutting between soul and spirit, between joint and marrow. It exposes our innermost thoughts and desires. Nothing in all creation is hidden from God. Everything is naked and exposed before his eyes, and he is the one to whom we are accountable."

What does it say God's Word is? _____

When you open God's Word, your Bible, do you feel as if Someone just stepped into the room? I do. Because Someone just did. That's the presence of the Lord. I find that exciting.

What else does it say in verse 12 about the word of God? _____

_____

God's Word cuts to the deepest recesses in our bodies, *cutting between soul and spirit, between joint and marrow*. God sees everything about us, yet still loves us deeply. Though we wear clothes, we are exposed naked before Him. Does that make you feel vulnerable? It does me.

But although we are exposed before God, He sees everything we do and we are accountable for everything we have ever said, thought (even the hateful things we have thought), done, or experienced, God *still* wants to do a great work in us and with us. Remember, Jesus experienced the same challenges. He understands our hurt, anger, sorrow, sickness, depression, abuse, everything. There is nothing you can name right now that Jesus does not understand. You are not alone. You are not left out.

You may be wondering what all this has to do with discovering your true identity. It has everything to do with it, because you have to know the why and the what-for of the things you're experiencing in order to push back the veil of your identity. Let's keep moving forward.

Read Psalm 33:13-15.

Where does the LORD look from? _____

What does He see? _____

From where does He observe? _____

Write verse 15 on the following lines: _____

_____

What does He understand and why? _____

_____

If God made us, He definitely understands everything about us, what we do, and our motivations. He knows us from the inside out. So why is it so hard for us to understand or even believe that He has a great and wonderful plan for us?

Look again at the first part of John 10:10 then write what it says below.

_____

Now read Psalm 32:7-8.

What does the psalmist write that God is? _____

What does He protect us from? _____

He is our hiding place and He protects us from trouble. But then He goes one step further. What does it say in the last part of verse 7? _____

_____

By surrounding us with songs of victory, wouldn't that tell you that He brings deliverance? I think so. That's a link to discovering your identity. You are *delivered*. So even though our enemy, the devil, comes to steal, kill, and destroy, God surrounds us with songs of victory.

Now look at verse 8. Once we are delivered, what does the LORD say He will do?

_____

There is never a moment when God isn't leading, guiding, advising, and watching over you. Therefore, another link in discovering your identity is realizing you are smart and can learn. In other words, you are *teachable*.

Debriefing:
So far in this journey we have learned that in order to discover our true identity we must be brought back from the dead. We need to have life breathed back into us. We need to be rescued from the Valley of Dry Bones, to rise up from the ashes. We also need the Holy Spirit. We can no longer afford to lie in the dust or hide in fear. There is no place for either.

Arise, dear ones, we are only beginning.

Be sure to journal what stood out to you in this chapter and don't forget to turn to the **Who I Am in Christ page***, and write the two links you found.*

Dry bones... come to life
Ezekiel 37:4-6

*ponder * pray * journal*

Week Two

Battle Lines

Every soldier must know, before he goes into battle, how the little battle he is to fight fits into the larger picture, and how the success of his fighting will influence the battle as a whole.
- Bernard Law Montgomery, www.brainyquote.com, soldier in battle

Even before time began, battle lines were drawn. It started in heaven when Lucifer decided he could be as great as or greater than God. Of course, God stepped over those lines and *like lightning* Lucifer fell. Now, where most people get confused is when they refer to Lucifer, aka Satan, as coming from hell. He's not there. When Lucifer fell, he fell to earth. I would imagine he fell with a mighty big *thud*. And that is where we will find our battle lines today.

God knew the larger picture before He ever created time. He knew, yet He chose, to proceed with Creation, time, even you and me. We ask why, yet we cannot see the bigger picture. Only God can see it. It must be a pretty awesome picture for Him to continue to allow us to wake up every morning and do the things we do. The enemy still threatens, attacks, and tries to destroy God's plans. Let's look at one of his most famous attacks.

Read Genesis 3:1 below, from the Amplified Bible.

"NOW THE serpent was more subtle and crafty than any living creature of the field which the Lord God had made. And he [Satan] said to the woman, 'Can it really be that God has said, You shall not eat from every tree of the garden?'"

Notice what it says about the serpent in the verse above, then fill in the blanks below. "...that he was more _____ and _____ than any living creature of the field."

Described as subtle and crafty and disguised as a snake, Satan doesn't spark fear into Eve. Instead, he spawns confusion by questioning the very words of God, *"Can it really be that God has said...?"* If the devil can make you question God's word, he brings confusion into your life which can cause you to say and do things contrary to, or opposite of what God's perfect plan for you truly is. Hence, Eve eating of the forbidden fruit and Adam doing likewise.

When we disobey God's instructions, we begin to venture away from Him and eventually find ourselves out of His will. Once we do, the enemy begins to whisper into our minds negative, derogatory comments and soon we question God's love for us. But he doesn't use his own words. He will use our own.

I've done too many bad things.
God is mad at me.
I can't serve in church anymore.
I'm too old.
I have to get my life straightened out first.

What. A. Lie.

These are the battle lines we need to be aware of daily. Hear me out, lovely ones, I said *daily*. But if we know our enemy and his tactics, we can come against him swiftly, precisely, and victoriously.

Let's take a look at some true statements from God's Word and see if we can gain some counter measures.

Read 1 Corinthians 14:33 from the New King James Version, or NKJV.

"For God is not the author of confusion but of peace, as in all the churches of the saints."

If you feel confused, is it God who is causing it? _____

How do you know? _____

*What does this verse say God **is** the author of? _____*

Lack of peace should be one warning that the enemy may be attacking you. Confusion is another. God doesn't want us to be confused about Him or anything He has in His plans for us. He wants us to be at peace.

Don't stop there. Let's move on and see what other strategies we can uncover.

Read 2 Timothy 1:7 from the NKJV.

"For God has not given us a spirit of fear, but of power and of love and of a sound mind."

I find this passage particularly powerful and profound. In verses 3-6, the apostle Paul is writing to Timothy to give him encouragement. He is bringing to light Timothy's heritage and his faith, reminding him how his grandmother and his mother had raised him in trusting the Lord. Paul also reminds Timothy to stir up the gift of God within him through the laying on of his (Paul's) hands.

This gave me encouragement that even the saints of old dealt with the attacks of the enemy in much the same way that we have today.

*Look at verse 7 again. God does not give us **fear**. He gives us something better. Write them in the spaces provided. _____, _____ and a _____ _____*

And here we find three more links to your identity, dear ones. You are *powerful*, you have *love*, and you have a *sound mind*. We can even go as far as to add a fourth link and say you are *fearless*. Even though at times we do feel fear, the Bible says in many places that we should not be afraid.

God doesn't want us to be afraid, although it's a normal feeling. However, we also shouldn't operate according to our feelings. Instead, we should acknowledge our fear then move forward. Whatever we are preparing to do, we should do it even if we are afraid. When we do, we may find that our fears are unfounded and just another tactic of the enemy to prevent us from doing what God has called us to do.

Fear, feelings of powerlessness, confusion. These are areas where the enemy likes to poke. I say that because very often it feels as if we are being poked in sensitive areas. Now you have some positive weapons with which to counterattack the enemy when you feel that barb.

I think a big key to dealing with fear is to realize we won't ever be completely rid of it. Fear will often just show up unexpectedly. We must recognize it and deal with it right away. Be confident we have what it takes to deal with it, be active and never give up.

Let's look at a couple more counter-measures before we move on.

In the fourth chapter of the book of James, he, the author, talks about drawing close to God. One of the biggest countermeasures you can take against the devil is to stay as close to God as you possibly can.

Read James 4:7-8 from the Amplified Bible below.

"So be subject to God. Resist the devil [stand firm against him], and he will flee from you. Come close to God and He will come close to you. [Recognize that you are] sinners, get your soiled hands clean; [realize that you have been disloyal] wavering individuals with divided interests, and purify your hearts [of your spiritual adultery]."

What does it mean to subject ourselves to God? _____

_____

When we subject ourselves to God, we are merely making ourselves humble before Him. We respect Him. We love Him. That is *key* in coming against the devil.

What does verse 7 say next that we are to do? _____

How do we resist him (look at what the verse says in brackets)? _____

_____

When we resist the devil, what happens? _____

In the next verse, it says to come close to God. How does He then respond?

_____

Oftentimes we find ourselves having been disloyal to God, as the verse says. However, by realizing our mistake (humbling ourselves), we can reconnect with Him quickly.

Read James 4:10 from the NLT below.

"Humble yourselves before the Lord, and he will lift you up in honor."

What happens when we come to the Lord in humility? _____

_____

God wants to lift us up, to elevate us. That can mean more than just raising our spirits and making us feel better. God has such great big plans for us! The enemy wants to thwart those plans by constantly searching for our weak spots so he can attack us. He will poke, prod, pinch, and provoke in any and every area of our lives possible to cause us to stumble, get confused, distracted, angry, or ill.

How then, can we stay on top of things and ahead of the enemy? Let's look at one more counter measure.

> God wants to lift us up, to elevate us.

Read Ephesians 6:17 from the NLT.

"Put on salvation as your helmet, and take the sword of the Spirit, which is the word of God."

Salvation is our helmet. Armor is necessary at all times. We will cover wearing armor in another chapter, but how do we protect ourselves? Look at the second part of that verse. What does it say to take with us? _____

What is the sword of the Spirit? _____

God's Word, our Bible, is a sword. A mighty sword. Remember last week we talked about the Word of God being alive and powerful? It's not only powerful but sharp *(refer to Hebrews 4:12-13 in the last chapter)*. God's Word is very important not only in defeating our enemy, but in discovering our true identity.

By staying in the Word, we stay one step ahead of the devil at all times. How encouraging!

You may be wondering; *how can I stay in the Word* all *the time?* I understand. We all have things to do. It's life. But in the moments when we are between tasks, we can grab a couple of verses from the Word. In our quiet moments before we wake the kids (or the kids wake us!), we can grab the Bible and read. Or listen to worship music in the car.

Post some of your favorite verses throughout your house, car, and various other places so that wherever you go, God's Word is there. Talk to Him periodically throughout the day. Talk to Him as you lay your head down at night before you go to sleep.

The enemy has drawn the battle lines and he will entice you to cross over them many times. What if you were prepared beforehand and crossed the line ahead of him? Refer to James 4:7. Strategic planning is necessary and God is the best at strategy.

Every small battle we fight fits into God's bigger plan. We don't know the big plan, but He does. So, as we cross the battle lines daily we must be prepared. Let's take a look at how.

Realize You Have Authority.

> God has gifted you with spiritual authority.

As a child of God, a Christ follower, a Christian, God has gifted you with spiritual authority. But don't let that go to your head. You must keep your wits about you, dear Warrior Princess. Yet you cannot afford to be timid.

With authority comes responsibility. Maybe you don't want that responsibility. Or maybe you don't think you are ready. Regardless of whether we want that privilege or are ready for it, we still have it and it's up to us to use it in a way that brings glory to God.

So what do we do with this authority? What do we use it for? Oh, dear ones, this will be amazing to discover. When we talked about stepping over the battle lines, we are stepping directly into battle. Though our battles are not necessarily what we think they are. We are entering a very real but different realm.

Let's look at 2 Corinthians 10:3: "For though we walk in the flesh, we do not war according to the flesh" (NKJV).

We are human. We are going to have physical arguments, fights, and wars. However, those are because of spiritual warfare. We must realize that our war is in the supernatural; therefore, we must prepare spiritually.

Look up and read 2 Corinthians 10:4-6 (I used NKJV).

In every war weapons are used. What kind of weapons are ours? _____

What are the weapons to be used for? _____

_____

We talked earlier about battles being in our minds. What purpose do our spiritual weapons serve?

_____

When we take every thought captive, or bring our thoughts under control, we step over the battle lines of thoughts, emotions, and mental turmoil. In doing so, we are being obedient to the call God has on our lives. We can also help others become obedient with their thoughts and actions. This is where our authority comes to use.

In every battle, the enemy plots against you while you strategize on how to defeat him. Our enemy never stops. He never blinks (remember, he's like a snake and snakes have no eyelids). He creeps and prowls around, watching. We can never stop, either. We cannot put too much thought into our enemy because he uses the same tactics that he's used since the beginning. Therefore, we shouldn't have to think too hard in order to defeat him. We just need to pay attention and make sure our focus is on the Lord.

Read 1 Peter 5:8-9 below. I used the Amplified Bible because the added words give extra meaning and more description to the instruction. Then answer the questions.

"Be well balanced (temperate, sober of mind), be vigilant and cautious at all times; for that enemy of yours, the devil, roams around like a lion roaring [in fierce hunger], seeking someone to seize upon and devour.
Withstand him; be firm in faith [against his onset – rooted, established, strong, immovable, and determined], knowing that the same (identical) sufferings are appointed to your brotherhood (the whole body of Christians) throughout the world."

What is the first thing we are told to do and for how long? _____

_____

For God to warn us to be on the alert at all times, don't you think it was for a reason?

Why should we be cautious at all times? _____

_____

With the devil continually stalking us, dear lovelies, we are a target. There are the battle lines again.

Why would we let our guard down for even one moment?

By reviewing the above text, how then do we protect ourselves?

_____

_____

We are given a little encouragement in also knowing that we aren't alone in being stalked by the enemy. All of our brothers and sisters in Christ deal with the same things we do. Though while we are going through those tough times, it often seems a lonely place to be.

Look up and read 1 Peter 5:7 and Psalm 55:2-3 (I used the Amplified Bible).

Though we go through many trials what does 1 Peter 5:7 say we should do about it?

_____

How much of our cares should we cast on the Lord? _____

Why do we do this? _____

In Psalm 55, what is the first thing that is asked of the Lord? _____

_____

In verse 3 of Psalm 55, whose voice is it that causes our distress? _____

We are a target for the enemy. He will use every means he can, including using other people, as a distraction to cause trouble for us. But there is always something we can do. Cry out to God.

When we cry out to God, He promises that He will be there for us.

Remember though, Jesus defeated our enemy, the devil, over two thousand years ago. Because of what Jesus did on the cross, Satan has no power. Although many give him power by allowing him to whisper lies over them, thereby they believe they are defeated. It's time to take a stand. It's time to begin asserting our spiritual authority.

Look again at 2 Corinthians 10:3 from the NLT.

"We are human, but we don't wage war as humans do."

Let me reiterate, our battle is not in the natural. It's in the spiritual. Therefore, we must be prepared spiritually for the battles we will face. Though sometimes people may be the ones who seem to be attacking us, remember, the enemy is behind the lines. He's in the background. But what do we do about the ones who say they, too, belong to Christ?

The apostle Paul addressed this subject in his letter to the Roman church, as he explained his own spiritual authority. His spiritual authority is also ours.

Read 2 Corinthians 10:7-8 below, from the NLT.

"Look at the obvious facts. Those who say they belong to Christ must recognize that we belong to Christ as much as they do. I may seem to be boasting too much about the authority given to us by the Lord. But our authority builds you up; it doesn't tear you down. So I will not be ashamed of using my authority."

According to the apostle Paul, from where does our authority come? _____

What does he say our authority does? _____

*What does it **not** do? _____*

Read Luke 10:18-20 from the NKJV.

"And He said to them, "I saw Satan fall like lightning from heaven.
Behold, I give you the authority to trample on serpents and scorpions, and over all the power of the enemy, and nothing shall by any means hurt you.
Nevertheless, do not rejoice in this, that the spirits are subject to you, but rather rejoice because your names are written in heaven."

What did Jesus give us authority over? _____

_____

What did He say could hurt us? _____

Even though the spirits are subject to us, because of our authority, what should we be most happy

about? _____

Knowing that we belong to Christ and our names are written in the Book of Life should be the most important thing to us. It should give us the most peace and happiness. Christ loves us; therefore, He would never allow anything to hurt us. That's why He gave us authority over all things, including the power of Satan, our enemy, which renders him powerless. Once we realize this, we can move forward in our journey of discovering our true identity and walking in the freedom Christ died for us to have.

Our spiritual authority not only comes from the Lord, it is meant to build each other up, not tear one another down. This is yet another link to our identity: we have ***spiritual authority***. Although we will encounter others who may seem to want to silence us, or maybe who don't understand the authority we claim, we cannot and should not be ashamed of the authority the Lord has given to us. Instead, we should walk in our authority humbly. This has great bearing on our identity and should also give us insight into the ploy of our enemy.

You must know the enemy is afraid of you. But he's not afraid of who you *were*. He doesn't care about your past, although he uses that against you to keep you tied up emotionally, mentally, spiritually, and yes, even physically, whenever he can. If he can keep you living in the past, you'll never move forward into your future, the one God has laid out for you.

No, lovelies, Satan is not afraid of who you *were*. He's afraid of *who you might become*. As a daughter of the Most High God, you were a threat upon conception. So the enemy began plotting against you, drawing those *battle lines*. He will even keep moving them to keep you from advancing, always trying to keep you behind the lines. He thinks he can prevent you from rising up into who God intended for you to be. However, once you realize who you are in Christ you become an even bigger threat to the enemy.

Therefore, we must learn to practice our authority and not allow ourselves to be dominated by our enemy, Satan. We must be trained in spiritual warfare. However, if we are always oppressed and dominated in the physical life, it will not feel normal to us to war in the spiritual. We will not possess the natural skill to war spiritually. This is why we must learn to use and exercise our spiritual weapons.

By understanding these battle lines, we can now move forward into discovering our role as a Warrior Princess and how to walk in that identity with confidence. We can also operate in a position of victory and help rescue and lead our sister warriors.

Debriefing:

In this part of our journey, we have studied how battle lines have been drawn since before time. Though we are human, we do not fight in the physical realm, but in the spiritual. We know that Satan draws the lines every day. He stalks us, always looking for ways to attack. We also learned God has declared us victorious! Even though we come under spiritual attack, our God-given authority can pull down strongholds, and should build up, not tear down. We should use it to help rescue and lead others to discover their identity in Christ.

Don't give up yet, lovely ones. Our story only gets more exciting!

Be sure to journal what stood out to you in this chapter, then turn to, **Who I Am in Christ** *page and write the links you found in this section.*

Battle is in the spiritual
2 Corinthians 10:3 (NLT)

ponder * *pray* * *reflect*

Week Three

Basic Training

"We are not transformed by rising to the occasion. We rise to the occasion because we have been transformed. How are we transformed? By the renewing of our mind. By convincing our heart that God is good, even when our circumstances are not."

-*Donna Partow*, This Isn't the Life I Signed Up *For (2003)*

When you accepted Jesus as Lord and Savior, you were immediately given an appointment, or assignment into the army of the Lord. Your *Basic Training* began, or rather, was to begin. You were given all the equipment necessary to carry out your mission.

However, not everyone understands the training. They may see the words on the page, but have a hard time understanding them or even believing them. We are *all* called. Though our assignments may differ greatly, yet they are still similar. How then, do we prepare for our assignment? We must re-train our brains. We must renew our minds. We must have Basic Training.

As in any branch of the military, the enlisted must be trained in the most basic of operations. They must learn discipline. They must learn the rules of the branch of the military they are in. They must learn how to listen to and respond to their commanding officer, and most importantly, how to strategize, fight, and win against the enemy. They also must learn how to operate in their specialized field.

The enlisted must retrain their brain to think and act like the soldiers they are. No longer are they civilians, but someone entirely different. Being a Warrior Princess in God's army, why would it be any different? As a daughter of the King, we do have privileges, as we studied in the last chapter. However, we do still need to be trained, always on the ready, always alert and always prepared. We cannot take our training lightly. It's important in discovering our identity.

In basic training the enlisted begin with the basics. So will we.

> Renewing our minds daily is essential in training.

Our brains need retraining. Now, I'm not talking about learning the rules of whatever denomination you are in. I'm talking about learning to hear and obey the LORD. That comes from reading His Word (the Bible). Our brains need to be given a refreshing and pure alternative to the everyday push of the world. Therefore, renewing our minds daily is essential in training.

Let's look at Romans 12:2 below from the Amplified Bible.

"And do not be conformed to this world [any longer with its superficial values and customs], but be transformed and progressively changed [as you mature spiritually] by the renewing of your mind [focusing on godly values and ethical attitudes], so that you may prove [for yourselves] what the will of God is, that which is good and acceptable and perfect [in His plan and purpose for you]."

The Amplified Bible gives a little more depth to the meaning of being renewed and why.

What do you think it means to conform? _____

_____

Instead of conforming to the world's standards, what are we to do? _____

_____

In what way are we to be transformed? _____

What should we focus on in order to be transformed? _____

In doing so, what do we prove and how? _____

Knowing we have an enemy constantly stalking us, looking to destroy, should keep us focused on godly values and ethical attitudes. We need continual renewing of our minds in order to stay prepared and ready to defeat him. That means renewing every day.

A key strategy is to memorize Scripture. In doing so, we always have the Word with us and in us. That is powerful stuff, lovelies.

Read Psalm 119:11 below, from the NLT.

"I have hidden your word in my heart, that I might not sin against you."

What purpose does it serve to hide God's Word in our hearts? _____

_____

Keeping the Word in our hearts helps prevent us from sinning. However, we are not perfect. We *will* mess up. We don't always do it on purpose, but it happens. When we do make a mistake, the enemy will use that to bring an attack against us. Yet the Holy Spirit helps us in bringing the Word to mind so we can open our mouth and speak the Word, defeating the enemy again.

Our training is preparedness for when the devil will whisper lies into our minds and for when we encounter temptations that bring us to the point of decision. Though the devil cannot hear our thoughts, he doesn't have to know them. All he's concerned with is getting you to believe *his* lies. Remember, the battlefield is often our minds.

Even Jesus dealt with enemy attack. How He handled it was to speak out loud, directly to the devil. By using His example, we can do likewise.

Look up and read Matthew 4:1-11 (I used NKJV). Then answer the questions below.

What was the purpose of Jesus being in the wilderness? _____

_____

How did He get there? _____

List the three ways Satan tempted Jesus. _____

_____

_____

Jesus answered Satan each time He was tempted. What were the first three words Jesus said each time?

" _____ _____ _____ "

After He said those words, Jesus quoted God's Word back to Satan. By the third time, how did Satan

respond? _____

What happened after he left Jesus? _____

God laid out the strategy for defeating the enemy long ago. Jesus showed us how to use it. It's up to us to follow through.

The enemy uses the same three tactics today as he did when he tempted Jesus. He will use our physical needs, emotional needs, and our pride or desire for significance or power to cause us to slip. If he can succeed, he will then begin the attacks in our minds, trying to convince us that God no longer loves us, needs us, or wants us. If we believe the lies, we slip further into the pit of self-pity, self-loathing, and isolation. This is why training is so very important, along with staying close to our brothers and sisters in Christ.

Often God will allow us to be tempted in order to test our loyalty to Him. Don't misunderstand, God does not cause bad things to happen to us. Though He does *allow* it in order to either make a point with you or with someone around you.

> God laid out the strategy for defeating the enemy long ago. Jesus showed us how to use it.

Your faithfulness in such situations is crucial. For example, in the military when the troops go into various combat scenarios, they are training for the possibility of enemy attack. How they handle it prepares them and determines their ability. It helps them to grow as a soldier. They get stronger physically, mentally, and emotionally. Our training as a Warrior Princess is very similar, only add "spiritually" to that list.

How then, does this help us discover who we are in Christ? Knowing that even Jesus Himself was tempted by the devil gives us assurance that we are not alone. There is nothing we will face that Jesus hasn't faced. Because of His encounters and His suffering, He can comfort us, give us understanding, love, and support in everything we face.

Read the passage below out of 2 Corinthians 1:3-5 from the NLT.

"All praise to God, the Father of our Lord Jesus Christ. God is our merciful Father and the source of all comfort. He comforts us in all our troubles so that we can comfort others. When they are troubled, we will be able to give them the same comfort God has given us. For the more we suffer for Christ, the more God will shower us with his comfort through Christ."

Who is the source of all comfort? _____

In what does He comfort us? _____

What reason does it give that He comforts us? _____

Now look at verses 6 and 7 of the same passage:

"Even when we are weighed down with troubles, it is for your comfort and salvation! For when we ourselves are comforted, we will certainly comfort you. Then you can patiently endure the same things we suffer. We are confident that as you share in our sufferings, you will also share in the comfort God gives us."

When we go through troubles, God's Word says it's for our comfort and salvation. Though it may not make sense at the time, in our future encounters it will make perfect sense.

When we have been comforted during our suffering, what are we then able to do?

___

In this passage, we find another link to our identity. Though it may not seem like a piece of who we are, it's good to know we are **comforted** by God in all the things we go through. We don't go through anything alone. Not only does everyone go through trials and suffering, Jesus did as well.

Look up and read Hebrews 4:14-15 (I used NLT), then answer the questions below.

Who is our High Priest? _____

How do we know He understands our weaknesses, trials, and sufferings? _____

___

Look at verse 16. How does it say we can now come to the throne of grace? _____

What will we receive? _____

What will we find and when? _____

When we need it most, we will find grace to help us when we come boldly before God and receive His mercy. He is there for us. *Always.* He is our Commander in Chief; therefore, we should always follow His directions because they are always given in love and for our benefit.

As women, you and I are important to God. We have been since before time. If we look back in Genesis, God even said, *"It is not good for the man to be alone. I will make a helper who is just right for him"* (Genesis 2:18, NLT). This isn't a sexist or racist remark. It's truth. God created woman to be the helper to man, to come alongside him and be one with her husband. Man, and woman are a team. When they both have a relationship with Jesus, together, they are a powerful force to be reckoned with. They are a dual threat to the enemy.

Since the beginning, the devil has been trying to drive a wedge between man and woman, husband and wife. He started in the Garden of Eden and who did he zero in on? The woman. This is why it is very important for us as women to discover our true identity and train for the battles ahead. We can't allow ourselves to be deceived by our enemy any longer.

This is not to say if you're a single woman, by choice or for any reason, that you aren't important. *All* women are important. However, married or single, the enemy is out to destroy and undermine women, their purpose, and their ministry. Women have been oppressed for centuries. Controlled, sold into various forms of slavery; physical, sexual, even mental and emotional. There are many children, young girls, and women sold into sex trafficking every day. There are also many who are being rescued daily because the ones who have found their freedom are rising up and going into battle to free these precious souls.

Even as you read this, God is freeing women all over the world, not just from human trafficking, but from depression, drug abuse, prostitution, gambling, pornography addiction, physical abuse and much more. He is elevating women to new and exciting heights. When God frees you of something that has kept you in bondage or slavery, it's exhilarating. Once free, it is important to retrain and renew your mind in order to use your story to help free someone else who suffers in the bondage you were once held captive.

Whatever it is that controlled you, God wants you to use your story to help another. He has chosen you to bring that good news to unshackle the chains holding someone else down. You could be the key that Jesus uses to unlock their chains.

Maybe you don't think you're qualified. Maybe you aren't sure you have what it takes. You may wonder if God even knows who you are. There were also people in the Bible who felt that way, unsure they were qualified or that God knew them, much less called them to do something specific for Him.

Read what the Lord said to the prophet Jeremiah from Jeremiah 1:5 below, out of the Amplified Bible. Though this was said to Jeremiah, it also applies to us today.

"Before I formed you in the womb I knew you [and approved of you as My chosen instrument], And before you were born I consecrated you [to Myself as My own]; I have appointed you as a prophet to the nations."

Now read Ephesians 1:4 from the NLT.

"Even before he made the world, God loved us and chose us in Christ to be holy and without fault in his eyes."

In the passages in Jeremiah and Ephesians, when do they say God knew us?

_____

Looking at Jeremiah 1:5, there are four things God said He did even before He knew us. List them below. I have given you the first one.

Approved, _____, _____, and _____ us.

In Ephesians 1:4, there are three more things God did for us. List them in the blanks.

He _____ us and chose us to be _____ and

_____ _____.

> We can't allow ourselves to be deceived by our enemy any longer.

We may have a hard time accepting this truth, however, dear ones, God not only knew us before He created us, He *chose* us. That's not all. The things we just wrote above are more links to our identity; **approved, chosen, consecrated (set apart), appointed, loved, holy, without fault (blameless).**

Though the enemy blasts accusations our way, God's Word says something very different. We were chosen long before the devil started accusing us. Because God loved us, He chose us to be holy and without fault. How can we be accused if we are blameless? This is why training is so important.

In basic training in the military, the enlisted have a schedule. They rise early, are required to meet together, they exercise together, learn together, work together, live together, and are expected to get along. Together. They are responsible for each other. The troops also learn the tactics of the enemy, how to identify him, how he speaks, acts, thinks, and even how to defeat him. The same training applies to us as God's children. We are responsible for each other. We will address this in the next chapter.

God set our training up long ago. Every saint (a person who has asked Jesus to be their Lord and Savior) before us had a purpose and an appointment to teach, preach, and write letters so that we would learn, grow and be able to carry on God's message to future believers. God isn't stupid, precious ones. Because He is omnipresent, He knew the end before the beginning. Therefore, He made a way for every generation, even you and me.

We *learn* from reading our Bibles. We *train* by listening to our pastors and teachers. There are many throughout our lives who have gone before us who will help lead, teach, and train us in our journey. Our job is to listen with open ears, mind, and heart, then ask the Lord to give us wisdom to discern the direction He wants us to take.

We will also encounter many who claim to be teachers, preachers, and prophets who are not. They will tell us things that aren't completely true. If we aren't properly trained, we will run the risk of being deceived and led down a destructive path. That's a dangerous place to be. But how do we know if what is being said to us is true?

Read the passage below out of 1 John 4:1-6 from **The Message** *version of the Bible.*

"My dear friends, don't believe everything you hear. Carefully weigh and examine what people tell you. Not everyone who talks about God comes from God. There are a lot of lying preachers loose in the world.

"Here's how you test for the genuine Spirit of God. Everyone who confesses openly his faith in Jesus Christ—the Son of God, who came as an actual flesh-and-blood person—comes from God and belongs to God. And everyone who refuses to confess faith in Jesus has nothing in common with God. This is the spirit of antichrist that you heard was coming. Well, here it is, sooner than we thought!

My dear children, you come from God and belong to God. You have already won a big victory over those false teachers, for the Spirit in you is far stronger than anything in the world. These people belong to the Christ-denying world. They talk the world's language and the world eats it up. But we come from God and belong to God. Anyone who knows God understands us and listens. The person who has nothing to do with God will, of course, not listen to us. This is another test for telling the Spirit of Truth from the spirit of deception."

To me, the above passage is very enlightening because I can see this unfolding in our world today. There are many who are standing before the masses, leading thousands into various things. The people are following along, blindly, believing that their leader is giving them the truth, causing them to rise up and stand for a cause when in reality they are being led into eventual destruction. This is not a political statement, nor is it race related. It's spirit-related. Plain and simple. How then, do we as Christ-followers get past this? This takes us back to basic training.

Look again at the passage above, 1 John 4:1-6.

What is the first thing the passage tells us to do? _____

After that, what are we to do **carefully***?* _____

How do we test for the genuine Spirit of God? _____

_____

There are two things that identify everyone who does not confess faith in Jesus. What are they?

1 _____

2 _____

There is one more test for discerning the Spirit of Truth from the spirit of deception. Can you name it? (the answer is in the last verse above)

_____

One more thing before we move on. In the passage above, it tells us who we come from and belong to. Look back at verse 4 and write the answer below.

_____

That, my dear beautiful sisters, should tell you more than you need to know. Not only do we *come from God*, we also **belong to God**. Therefore, anyone who tells you they know God should speak with and show love, not hate.

In the verse above, we also find another link to our identity. However, before we write it down, let's confirm it in another verse from God's Word.

Read Acts 17:28-29 from the NLT below.

"For in him we live and move and exist. As some of your own poets have said, 'We are his offspring.'
And since this is true, we shouldn't think of God as an idol designed by craftsmen from gold or silver or stone."

Who does it say we are? _____

There is the next link to your identity, dear ones. You are God's *offspring. His child. His daughter.* That is so exciting to me. Let's say this statement boldly, and out loud.

I AM THE DAUGHTER OF THE MOST HIGH GOD!

The Word says this is true. Therefore, since you are one of God's children, His offspring, how does that make you feel? Who is He to you? Write your thoughts below.

_____

_____

_____

_____

Debriefing:
We have come a long way in this chapter in discovering our true identity. It is not only important to renew our minds daily, but to also have good teachers in our lives who can help us in our basic training. We've learned where we come from and to whom we belong. We've also studied how to discern the Spirit of Truth from the spirit of deception. Knowing these things gives us a good foundation so we can move further in our journey.

It's getting more exciting, lovelies. Let's move forward.

Be sure to journal what stood out to you in this chapter, then turn to **Who I Am in Christ,** *and write the links you found in this section.*

Be transformed

ponder * pray * journal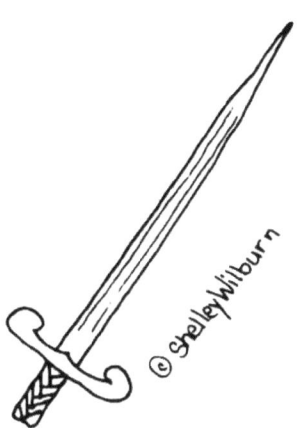

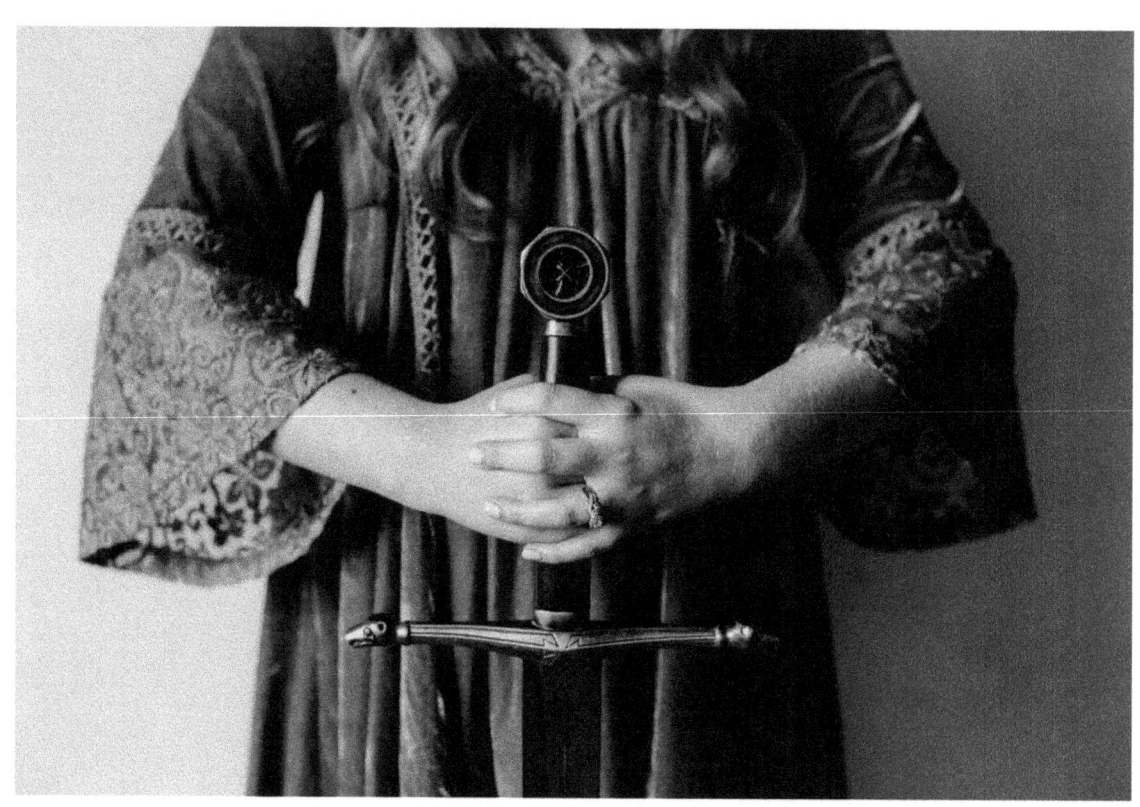

Week Four

Your Assignment

"Whatever God shows you to do – obey it quickly."
  - Rich Mendola, "Joy in the Holy Spirit…in the Desert" sermon (2009),
  [The Complete Guide to Christian Quotations, pg. 320]

By now, lovely ones, you have a growing list of adjectives describing who you are as God's precious one. Not only are you all those things, but so much more.

In this chapter, our journey takes us even deeper into discovering more about who God says we are. Along with what we've already uncovered we will add more and more to our list in the back of the book.

Being a Warrior Princess, one of God's chosen, His offspring, we discover that we all have an assignment. Some say it's our calling. Others call it our mission. Nevertheless, whatever we name it, assignment, calling, mission, hopes and dreams, desires, it's still an assignment and it comes from God. What we do with it depends on our obedience to Him as our Heavenly Father.

Each of us has been given a place in God's agenda. That should tell you how important you are to Him. Each one of us is part of God's wonderful, amazing, larger-than-life plan. We all have a call on our lives. We have all been given special talents and abilities and are expected to use them to help and encourage others in this life journey.

Regardless of our individual talents and abilities, our assignment is that we are all called to restore the people of God to a right relationship with Him. We are called to encourage, inspire, build up, heal, nurture, teach, and yes, even to warn our sisters in Christ. By warn, that doesn't mean to tear down, insult, ridicule, or mock. A loving word from a sister in Christ, a sister Warrior Princess, is what our sisters who are in bondage need.

Let's dive right into discovering what our assignment is and how we are to carry it out. In the process, look for more links into your identity, dear hearts.

Going back into the book of Ezekiel, look at what God tells the prophet in Ezekiel 33:7-9 from the NLT.

"Now, son of man, I am making you a watchman for the people of Israel. Therefore, listen to what I say and warn them for me.

If I announce that some wicked people are sure to die and you fail to tell them to change their ways, then they will die in their sins, and I will hold you responsible for their deaths.

But if you warn them to repent and they don't repent, they will die in their sins, but you will have saved yourself."

> "Now, son of man, I am making you a watchman for the people of Israel. Therefore, listen to what I say and warn them for me."
> ~Ezekiel 33:7 (NLT)

Those are some pretty strong words. Though they were spoken many years ago, they are still just as powerful and relevant and apply even to us today. There is also a link into our identity. It is found in verse 7. We, as Warrior Princesses, have been appointed as **watchmen** for our sisters in Christ. A big responsibility, yes. However, it does not negate who we are, nor does it mean we can use our authority for personal gain.

In the verses above, who is Ezekiel a watchman for? _____

_____

What assignment does God give Ezekiel to do? _____

_____

If he fails to warn them, who does God hold responsible? _____

If he does warn the people, what will happen? _____
_____

God never promises that when we bring a message to our sisters they will listen. However, if we fail to do what God has given us to do and one of our sisters falls into peril, then we *are* responsible.

Before we delve deeper into that, let's look a little more into our assignment to get a better understanding of what God has called us to do.

Look up Jeremiah 1:5-12 (I used NLT). Then answer the questions below.

Where did the LORD tell the prophet Jeremiah to go? _____
_____

What did He tell Jeremiah to say? _____

The LORD gave Jeremiah some profound instructions in verses 1-7. Then, in verse 8, He began to reassure Jeremiah. What did He say?

_____

_____

How did Jeremiah know what he was supposed to say? _____
_____

When the LORD showed Jeremiah the branch from the almond tree, what did that mean?
_____

God is always watching. He will also always carry out all of His plans. Regardless of whether we are obedient, God's plans never fail and His message will be delivered one way or another. It would be prudent for us as His daughters to carry out the message He gives us regardless of the repercussions we may *think* we'll incur from those around us.

I personally would rather give a difficult message to a sister in Christ and risk *her* retaliation than to keep my mouth shut and be held responsible for her actions because I didn't deliver a message from our heavenly Father.

Please note, lovelies; God is not mad at you, nor is He waiting for you to mess up so He can zap you into oblivion. Sweet, sweet, sisters, our God is a loving Father and even if we do mess up and neglect to speak when the Holy Spirit prompts us to speak, God still loves us and will use us for His glory if we will come humbly to His throne of grace and repent of our mistakes because He's just that good. He's just that awesome.

But what if you do miss an opportunity? What if you miss an assignment? What then? Does God remove your calling?

Read Roman 11:29 from the NLT below.

"For God's gifts and his call can never be withdrawn."

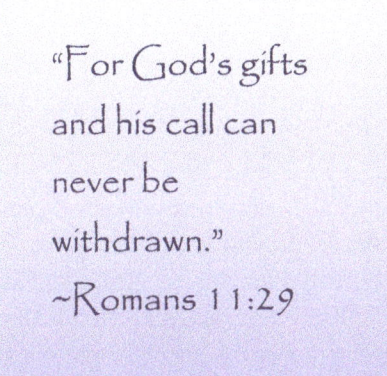

If we miss an opportunity, if we blatantly disregard an assignment from the Lord, it doesn't mean that we lose our gifts. They are still there. God doesn't make mistakes, dear ones. God doesn't make us obey. He doesn't bow to us or to what we want. He is perfect. He is sovereign. He knows exactly what He's doing. Our decision to disregard His instruction is not a surprise to Him. However, our choice to obey or disobey is strictly up to us. That's the beauty of free will. We can choose what we want to do. Our decision will also either grant us a blessing or cause us to miss a blessing.

Read Isaiah 55:11 from the NKJV below.

"So shall My word be that goes forth from My mouth; It shall not return to Me void, But it shall accomplish what I please, And it shall prosper in the thing for which I sent it."

When God puts forth His Word, what happens to it? _____

_____

As a watchman, someone appointed (assigned) by God to warn the people of what He says, we have a great responsibility. Yet sometimes those we are assigned to speak to just won't listen. Sometimes the most difficult people to reach are the ones we are closest to.

Read Mark 6:4 from the NLT.

"Then Jesus told them, "'A prophet is honored everywhere except in his own hometown and among his relatives and his own family.'"

Our own family members may reject us because of our belief or our testimony. I have experienced this myself. For years I suffered severe depression, anxiety, and even verbal abuse from many sources. However, one day, I determined that I was done living in this way. I sought out healing from a God I wasn't sure would hear me. But He knew my heart and graciously placed wonderful, godly people in my path to help me (watchmen). Through His divine intervention, I was healed and no longer do I dwell in that ugly place.

My healing, while a miracle, is not accepted by everyone I meet or talk to. The words of Jesus ring true even with me. But that's okay. While it's a sad situation, I must press forward and do what God has called me to do. This is what you must do as well, dear sister sojourners, dear Warrior Princesses.

Though we don't carry out God's message for our honor, we also must realize that not everyone will hear our message, including family. We will then be presented with a decision. Stay quiet and stay in the good graces of family or friends who will not acknowledge our position? Or, follow a sovereign God who loves us more than the world?

Let's take a look at a sister who was placed in a high position and then presented with a life-and-death situation, not only for her family, but for herself. How she responds will mean life or death for all involved. Yet, she becomes deeply distressed about what to do.

Read Esther 3:8-13 and 4:1-14.

Esther, though queen, had a calling. But since she was distressed, what did her cousin Mordecai tell her in verse 14?
_____

_____

For such a time as this. Esther was placed in the palace with the king and found favor with him in such a way that he would do anything for her. Though she had a great enemy (Haman) and was even afraid and distressed because of the threat hanging over the lives of her people, her family and even herself, she was encouraged to take a stand and speak up. Her obedience saved a nation (read Esther, chapters 8-9).

We could learn a great lesson from Esther today. We are living in the time God has chosen for us. We have also been given a great calling for such a time as this. We will also come up against opposition. Remember in our previous chapters that we have a great enemy who will use every tactic to try to defeat us and keep us from the call God has on our lives. He will also do everything he can to prevent us from discovering our true identity.

So, what happens if we choose *not* to follow through with our call? There will also be times when we just blatantly go the opposite way when God gives us an assignment. What then? What happens when we do that? Know that God never gives up on us. He gives us every opportunity to do what's right. He will even go to the depths of the sea to get our attention.

If you read in the book of Jonah, the word of the LORD came to Jonah not once, but twice! Once, before he disobeyed and the second time after Jonah had spent three days and nights in the belly of the great fish.

Read Jonah 1:1-2 and Jonah 3:1-2 (I used the Amplified Bible).

Did God change His mind about what Jonah was to do? _____

Where did God tell Jonah to go the first time? _____

What were God's directions to Jonah the second time? _____

_____

God never changes His mind. His words to Jonah were the same. *"Arise, go to Nineveh, that great city…"* In chapter one it states to *"proclaim against it."* In chapter three, God says to *"preach and cry out to it."* Likewise, in chapter three, God said for Jonah to tell them what He, God, told him to say from chapter one. Therefore, God's word did not change.

When God gives you an assignment and you disobey, He will give you another chance to redeem yourself and be obedient to His call. However, if you still disobey, He may re-route that call to someone else to do, as we are about to see below. But please note, you are not condemned, lovely one – you just missed a blessing.

Read Judges 4:4-24 (I used NKJV).

Who was judging Israel at this time (the watchman)? _____

God chose Deborah to be in leadership position (the watchman) over Israel during this time period. While Israel was in captivity, God gave instructions for them to get out of captivity.

Who did Deborah relay those instructions to? _____

Was he obedient? _____

Because of his disobedience or lack of faith, what was Deborah's judgment?

_____

_____

Did Barak follow through with his assignment? What happened? _____

_____

Was Barak able to defeat Sisera and kill him? Who did? _____

_____

How did Sisera die and by whom? _____

_____

Deborah and Jael (pronounced *Yale*) are two examples of what can be done when we, as Warrior Princesses, stand and do what God has assigned us to do. Though Barak and the ten thousand men went against the army of Sisera and defeated them, Sisera fled and escaped. However, he did not live for long and was ultimately killed by Jael. Therefore, just as Deborah prophesied, Sisera was in fact killed by a woman.

This is not about being better than a man or doing a man's job—don't get me wrong. However, if we, meaning you and I, are called to do a job, not a man's job, it's ours. We all have our own special place and position in God's perfect plan. We are not in competition with each other, dear sisters. We are all working toward a common goal. We are placed in our time for a specific purpose and plan, ordained by God even before we were conceived.

The point of the story of Deborah, Barak, Sisera, and Jael is that when God gives you an assignment and you disobey or decline, He will see His plans through. He will find another who is willing to do what you would not. History is very important to learn and utilize. We can better not only ourselves, but our circumstances. Just because there has been depression, cancer, heart disease, addiction, or whatever your family has in its lineage, doesn't mean that it has to continue with you, or even your children or their children. Breaking generational curses, for example, is a very important part of our existence. We have that power and we should utilize every aspect of our assignment throughout our life walk.

Knowing what transpired before us is to teach us and encourage us in our journey. It will help us learn who we are in Christ and what our place is in God's plan. May we learn from those who have gone before us, through their trials and celebrations, through their victories and defeats.

Although we will have trials and opposition, we must remain confident that God knows what He's doing and therefore trust Him to give us the boldness and confidence to move forward. God is for us. We have nothing to fear.

Read Psalm 91:14 from the NLT below.

"The LORD says, 'I will rescue those who love me. I will protect those who trust in my name.'"

In this passage from Psalms, what does the LORD promise to do for those who love Him?

_____

If we trust Him, what has He promised? _____

There are two links to our identity, dear sisters. We are *rescued* and *protected* by God if we love and trust Him. But check out what it says in the next passage from 1 John below.

"For every child of God defeats this evil world, and we achieve this victory through our faith. And who can win this battle against the world? Only those who believe that Jesus is the Son of God." ~1 John 5:4-5 NLT

As a child of God, how do we defeat the world? _____

Who wins the battle against the world? _____

_____

We just discovered another link to our identity in Christ. We are *victorious*. If we love and trust God, we have nothing to worry or fear because He promises that we defeat the evil world. And we do it through our faith. Our faith makes us victorious.

Despite all the things the enemy throws at us, despite the people who would try to keep us in bondage, in the chains of our past, we can overcome that and be victorious just by having faith in Jesus and being obedient to the call God has on our lives.

Your story matters, dear one. No matter what you've been through or are going through now, you matter. You have a story to tell. You have a purpose and God has a plan. You cannot fail unless you refuse to stand. You are promised victory and so much more.

Read Romans 8:37 from the NLT below.

"No, despite all these things, overwhelming victory is ours through Christ, who loved us."

What type of victory does it say is ours? _____

Now look how the New King James words it below:

"Yet in all these things we are more than conquerors through Him who loved us."

Overwhelming victory. The New King James Version says "more than a conqueror." With statements like that, how can we not step out into our calling?

There is another link to your identity, lovely ones; you are a *conqueror*, an *overcomer*.

Through Christ, who loved us, still loves us, will always love us, we can have the confidence and assurance that we will succeed in whatever it is God has called us to do. We just need to step out in faith and obedience.

We talked earlier about our being God's children, His offspring, but that isn't all.

Look up Romans 8:17 and write it below (I used NLT).

_____

_____

_____

Not only are we God's children, what does the above passage say we are? _____

_____

Because of Jesus, we share His inheritance. In that passage, we find another link to our identity. We are an *heir*. In addition to our shared inheritance with Jesus, our Brother, in order to share in His glory, we must also share the suffering.

Some may find this tough to accept or believe. Therefore, not everyone will listen to or accept what we have to say. Some will not believe in Him, nor will they believe in our healing, our story, or the blessings He has bestowed upon us. Some, in their own grief or struggles, will not be able to understand a God who loves them unconditionally because they have been blindsided by the enemy.

It all ties together and it ultimately points us directly back to Jesus. We just have to be willing to look, listen, and obey.

After knowing all the things our assignment can bring us, opposition, resistance, battle, etc., how, then, can we defend ourselves? We must be prepared at all times. We will look at that in the next chapter. Get ready, dear Warrior Princesses…it's time to suit up!

Debriefing:

In this chapter, we have studied how each of us has a call on our lives. We discovered we have been appointed watchmen over our siblings, called to give them inspiration and encouragement, but also warnings to help them come back to the Lord. We have also learned that our gifts and callings are irrevocable and that even when we miss our call, we can repent and be back in a right relationship with God. Not only that, but we have also discovered not everyone will be receptive to who we are in Christ yet we still have an assignment and God gives us a choice.

Be sure to journal what stood out to you in this chapter and write all the links to your identity on the Who I Am in Christ page.

Perhaps you were made for such a time as this

Esther 4:14

I am a watchman
Ezekiel 33:7

*ponder * pray * reflect*

Week Five

Prepare for Battle

"This is not suggested; it is commanded. The Bible would not have told us to take up the whole armor of God in order to withstand evil if evil could have been withstood without doing that."
— Stormie Omartian, topfamousquotes.com

In every branch of the military the troops have a uniform. In fact, they have more than one. They have the everyday uniform they wear when doing their everyday tasks. They have the combat uniforms. And they have their dress uniforms when performing formal duties or attending formal events.

Each piece of the uniform has a specific purpose and meaning. The uniform is not complete unless every piece is worn from head to toe. To leave out a piece of the uniform, the soldier would be considered out of uniform and therefore unprotected.

As a Warrior Princess, we too have a uniform we wear. We call it armor. We are to wear it at all times, day and night. Our armor is a custom fit, yet one size fits all. Your physical size does not matter. God has armor specially designed to fit you. The best thing about our armor is it's stylish and never goes out of fashion nor is it ever outdated. It goes with everything.

Up to this point we have discussed many aspects of our identity as Warrior Princesses, God's chosen, appointed ones. We know that through many circumstances we can become dry bones, hardly alive, yet Jesus wants to breathe life back into us. He wants us to receive the Holy Spirit, who will help us not only in our journey but in discovering who we are in Christ.

We also know that before time began the battle lines were drawn and war was waged upon God's creation: us. We have identified our great enemy, the devil, aka Satan, and know that he hates us because he hates God. Therefore, he wants nothing more than to steal, kill, and destroy us and everything about us.

However, we also know that we can be prepared for the enemy's attacks. By renewing our minds, changing how we look at the world around us, and by remembering that our fight is not in the natural but the spiritual, we have a head start in overcoming the attacks of the enemy.

Perhaps one of the most important things we can do to be prepared is to make sure we have on the *whole* armor of God. *All of it.* We must constantly be covered from head to toe if we are to protect ourselves from the onslaught of the enemy. It wouldn't do for the troops to go into battle without their battle gear on, their protective covering, so why should we, as Warrior Princesses, be any different?

> One of the most important things we can do to be prepared is to make sure we have on the whole armor of God.

Let's begin by looking at why we wear the armor in the first place.

Read Ephesians 6:10-11 from the NLT below, then answer the questions.

> *"A final word: Be strong in the Lord and in his mighty power.*
> *Put on all of God's armor so that you will be able to stand firm against all strategies of the devil."*

How much of the armor are we to put on? _____

When we wear all of God's armor, does it say we will weak or strong? In what?

_____

Why put on all of the armor? _____

_____

Prepare for Battle

If we have on armor, then we are preparing for battle. But what kind of battle are we preparing for? Who or what are we fighting against?

_____

Read Ephesians 6:12 below, from the NLT, then write your answer on the lines provided.

"For we are not fighting against flesh-and-blood enemies, but against evil rulers and authorities of the unseen world, against mighty powers in this dark world, and against evil spirits in the heavenly places."

_____

_____

_____

> No soldier goes into battle unprepared.

We studied in the previous chapters that the enemy is constantly on the lookout for someone to attack. The exact words are "someone to devour." With an enemy like that, it would behoove us to be on the ready. We cannot afford to let our guard down.

No soldier goes into battle unprepared. To do so would be life-threatening or even fatal. Why then, would we not wear our spiritual armor at all times? As God's Warrior Princess, we must be ready, always prepared whether we are in the lull or in the throes of all out spiritual attack.

In the verse below, you will find the reason why we should wear all of God's armor. Write the reason on the lines following the verse.

"Therefore, put on every piece of God's armor so you will be able to resist the enemy in the time of evil. Then after the battle you will still be standing firm." ~Ephesians 6:13 (NLT)

_____

_____

After the battle is over, where will we be? _____

In all the things we've learned up until now, one thing we have been assured of is that we will be victorious, more than a conqueror, still standing firm.

We cannot go into battle with our great enemy without knowing how he operates, or how we can and should respond to him. We must also protect ourselves from enemy attack if we are going to still be standing when the battle is over. This is why armor is so very important.

As God's Warrior Princess, though we are more than conquerors, we must still be ready for attack every second of every day. It cannot be stressed enough. Sure, we let our guard down at times. Yet it is at those times when the enemy takes advantage of our situation to slither in and place doubt, confusion, fear, and even enmity between us and those we love. He doesn't come in from the front lines where we can see him. He will slide in between the cracks in our armor and whisper his lies. This is why we must always be prepared for battle, especially in our minds. Every piece of armor a soldier, or Warrior Princess, wears has a purpose. No piece is any less effective than the other. They all serve their purpose in protecting every part of the wearer and all work together to ensure the best protection when worn together.

Begin to put on your armor by reading the list from Ephesians 6:14-17 below, from the NLT (emphasis is mine).

> *"Stand your ground, putting on the **belt of truth** and the **body armor of God's righteousness**. For **shoes**, put on the **peace** that comes from the Good News so that you will be fully prepared. In addition to all of these, hold up the **shield of faith** to stop the fiery arrows of the devil. Put on **salvation** as your **helmet**, and take the **sword of the Spirit**, which is the **word of God**."*

In the very first part of this passage, before putting on our armor, we are instructed to do what?

_____

As we stand our ground we are to begin putting on our armor. On the lines below, list each piece of armor and its use.

Piece of Armor	Use
_____	_____
_____	_____
_____	_____
_____	_____
_____	_____
_____	_____

Remember, Satan fights with lies. Sometimes the lies of the enemy will sound like truth because it may make sense in our minds, but that's where this slimy snake attacks us. We must make sure we know God's truth. We should wear it like a belt around our waist, protecting us.

Any time we are presented with information we must always compare it to God's Word. Does it line up with what the Word says? If it doesn't, it's a lie. Only believers have God's truth and only God's truth can defeat Satan's lies.

But how do we know the difference between God and the devil? Maybe you feel this way at times. You aren't sure if what you're thinking or feeling is God or the enemy and you're just a little bit confused. Therefore, how can we truly know?

Read below what 1 Corinthians 14:33 says, from the ESV.

"For God is not a God of confusion but of peace. As in all the churches of the saints..."

You're feeling confused? What does the Word above say about confusion?

_____

If God is not the author of confusion, what is He the author of? _____

Is God causing your confusion, then…? _____

God is the author of *peace*. If you don't have peace, then my dear, you are being attacked by the devil, who loves to twist God's Word into something vile and malicious. He loves to lie to you.

In the book of John, Jesus is teaching in the temple and the Pharisees begin questioning Him, trying to trap Him into saying something wrong so they can condemn Him. But Jesus already knows their hearts and their motives and He calls them out on their lies and where they're getting their lies.

Look at John 8:41b-44 from the NKJV below.

"…Then they said to Him, "We were not born of fornication; we have one Father – God."

Jesus said to them, "If God were your Father, you would love Me, for I proceeded forth and came from God; nor have I come of Myself, but He sent Me.

Why do you not understand My speech? Because you are not able to listen to My word.

You are of your father the devil, and the desires of your father you want to do. He was a murderer from the beginning, and does not stand in the truth, because there is no truth in him. When he speaks a lie, he speaks from his own resources, for he is a liar and the father of it."

Who did Jesus say the Pharisees' father was? _____

What did Jesus say the devil is and has been from the beginning? _____

_____

In the last sentence, who did Jesus say the devil is? _____

_____

The devil never tells the truth. Therefore, he is nothing more than a murderer and a liar. He is the father of lies. So, when we say we should put on the belt of truth and the body armor of God's righteousness, God's Word is our truth. When we saturate ourselves with Scripture (verses from the Bible) we are covering ourselves with His protection against the lies of the enemy.

Let's finish putting on our armor.

Wearing God's righteousness as your breastplate protects your heart because that's where we keep our emotions, self-worth and trust and that's where the enemy often attacks. We are assured of God's approval of us within our hearts. He approves of us because He loves us. We know this because He sent His Son, Jesus, to die for us.

The next part of our armor is shoes. What Warrior Princess doesn't love shoes? These shoes are, as a friend of mine puts it, "da bomb-diggity." They are shoes of peace.

Wearing shoes of peace means, as we travel, spreading the Good News of Jesus to those needing encouragement, we are bringing peace.

The enemy wants us to think trying to reach people for Christ is worthless and hopeless. He wants us to think the size of our task is too big and the negative responses will be too much to handle. I know, dear sister warriors, I experience it every day, too. Many are the times I've had that imaginary conversation with someone, anyone, who would probably not listen to what I had to say, or invariably argue with me. But that never transpires.

Our shoes of peace God gives us are the motivation to continue to spread the true peace that only comes from God. Everyone needs to hear it.

Having a shield of faith is extremely important while we are suiting up. Our faith guards us and protects us from enemy attack. Satan likes to throw accusations, insults, setbacks, temptations, and much more at us like fiery darts. Our faith acts as that shield, deflecting the fiery darts the enemy fires at us. They may hit, but those fiery darts, fiery arrows, will hit our faith and literally bounce off, proving us unaffected by his attacks.

I'm speaking from personal experience here. You can read about that in my book, *Walking Healed*, for a more in-depth look at healing and how the enemy tries to sabotage us with his fiery darts.

While we know that wearing the breastplate of righteousness protects us against the enemy's attacks on our hearts, we also must wear the helmet of salvation to protect our minds. Many women today are being attacked by depression, anxiety, fear, and things that they dwell on by thinking daily, worrying about the *what ifs* in their lives. Lovely, beautiful sister warriors, this is the oldest trick of the devil!

The enemy will whisper such lies into our minds that once the fear begins, it snowballs into an avalanche that can paralyze us into immobility, preventing us from moving forward into our calling. That's exactly what the devil was going for.

The helmet is a very important piece of armor. It protects the head from injury. In ancient times, the helmet covered more than just the head. It wrapped around the face, protecting the cheeks, eyes, and nose. It was also elongated and covered the neck on the sides and back. It didn't prevent an attack, just helped protect from a major blow from behind or from the sides. Many opponents carried swords, wielding them at will, trying to strike the most tender area, the neck. If an opponent could strike the neck, it would be fatal for the soldier.

A physical helmet protects the head, face, ears and neck. The helmet of salvation, a spiritual piece of armor, protects our minds from the lies of the enemy. It should remind us of our security in Christ. When the enemy comes, whispering words to bring fear, confusion, and doubt, we can combat with the security that our salvation produces. Salvation is more than just a ticket into heaven. Those beautiful minds of ours are protected, keeping us reminded of exactly who and Whose we are.

We aren't done with armor yet. You may have noticed there is an extra line in the listing of the armor. There is still one piece of armor left, which people often miss when reading about putting on the whole armor. Read on, dear warriors, for the most important piece of protection going into battle.

Look at Ephesians 6:18 below from the NLT, then turn back to the list of armor on the previous pages and fill in the blank.

"Pray in the Spirit at all times and on every occasion. Stay alert and be persistent in your prayers for all believers everywhere."

Prayer. So very important. Prayer is us seeking a Holy God for our protection, deliverance, salvation, and success. Prayer shows the Lord that we trust Him. Like talking to your best friend every day, your relationship grows ever closer. It's the same way with the Lord. Praying, talking to Him every day will make your relationship with Him even stronger.

Praying in the Spirit engages the Holy Spirit to give us direction, come to our aid, give us protection, and guide our every step in battling the enemy. Remember, the enemy is already defeated. However, he never gives up. Therefore, we must always be persistent in our prayers. They keep us in a right relationship with God. Our prayers also remind our enemy, the devil, that he has no power.

Looking back at Ephesians 6:18, how often does it say we are to pray in the Spirit and when?

_____

In the last part of that verse what does the apostle Paul say regarding how we should conduct our prayers and whom we should include?

_____

> No soldier goes into battle without being alert.

No soldier goes into battle without staying alert. Letting down your guard can prove destructive or even fatal. In the spiritual, we cannot afford to sit idly by, not paying attention. We must stay alert. By staying alert, we keep ourselves always at the ready.

Read Matthew 7:7-8 below from the NLT.

"Keep on asking, and you will receive what you ask for. Keep on seeking, and you will find. Keep on knocking, and the door will be opened to you.
For everyone who asks, receives. Everyone who seeks, finds. And to everyone who knocks, the door will be opened."

Jesus says we are to keep doing what? _____

What happens when we continue to:

   Ask _____

   Seek _____

   Knock _____

Who is this for? _____

I'm so glad we can talk to God all the time and tell Him everything on our minds and hearts, aren't you?

We have come so far already, dear ones. But we aren't done yet. Now that we are suited up with our armor on, prayed up, standing our ground, we are ready for battle. Keeping that ever-fashionable armor on at all times keeps us on the ready. It also lets the enemy know that we know who we are and Whose we are.

Notice we haven't yet had any links to our identity in this chapter. We are laying ground for more to come. We have already written many links to who God says we are. You should have a pretty good idea beginning to float around in your beautiful heads. Now wrap it up in your armor and keep it protected.

Though we have studied the importance of wearing our armor continually, it may begin to concern some of you about the actual battle you must face. Every battle is different. Although we are called to the battle frontline, we don't have to fear. We won't battle alone. We are never alone dear, warrior sisters. Though the enemy tries to send fear, confusion, and distraction our way, if we'll keep our wits about us,

God will show us amazing and wonderful things.

Throughout the Bible, God has strategically placed prior events to encourage us and embolden us to step onto the battle ground just as our ancestors before us. Once we have all our armor on and are prayed up, all we have to do is stand. Did you hear me, lovely ones? I said, *stand*. Stand and watch the Lord fight for you. He has promised that.

When Moses led the children of Israel out of Egypt and they came to the Red Sea, they felt hopeless. They had this great body of water before them and the army of Pharaoh quickly gaining on them. But God parted the sea so they could cross on dry land. However, though they crossed, Pharaoh's army followed. I imagine I would have been as terrified as they were, yet God took care of things, just like He promised.

Read Exodus 14:13-14 below from the Expanded Bible (EXB).

"But Moses answered, "Don't be afraid! Stand still and you will see the LORD save you today. You will never see these Egyptians again after today.
You only need to remain calm [or still]; the LORD will fight for you."

One of the most important things we can do when facing battle, Moses mentions first in verse 13. Write it in all capital letters below.

_____ _____ _____.

Fear is one of the first things that seems to happen when faced with adversity, isn't it? But God tells us throughout the Bible, "Don't be afraid," even in the most terrifying circumstances. He wouldn't have put it in there if He didn't mean it.

Looking back at the previous verses, what was the next thing Moses told the people to do?

_____

When God says to stand still, He's getting ready to do something amazing. It was no different during this time. Moses told the people to stand still and watch. Watch as the LORD saves you.

Say what?

The LORD is going to save me? Yes! I can literally answer that with a resounding *YES!* because I, too, am one of the saved ones. And there is another link to your identity: you are *saved*. You are rescued. Oh, dear ones, if you could but see and realize how precious you are to Him. Though you are a Warrior Princess, you are also a child of the Most High God. He loves you. He cherishes you. He adores you.

So why do bad things happen?

Therein lies the million-dollar question. Because we live in a fallen world, because there is evil in our world, there are so many today who are living below their means. I'm not talking about poverty, although that's also one of the issues. I'm talking about oppression, depression, anxiety, human trafficking, drug abuse, sexual abuse, physical abuse, addictions, and so many other things that are preventing our precious sisters, God's precious daughters, from living the full, abundant life He created for them.

You may be wondering how that affects you. Maybe you think it doesn't affect you. But it does. Remember, in the previous chapter we discussed that we are Watchmen. We are called to go out and set the captives free. We are to warn our sisters. We are to help them. Therefore, we will ultimately do battle, not only for ourselves but for those who cannot battle for themselves. However, in that battle, I repeat, we do not fight alone. We must remember that and be encouraged. That should give all of us a little boost of confidence to press forward.

Debriefing:
In this chapter, we have discussed wearing the full armor of God and what function every piece of armor serves. We have also learned the enemy never stops in his attacks upon us and that we need to constantly be prepared for battle. However, we can rest assured that we won't have to battle alone because God will fight for us and save (rescue) us.

Be sure to journal what stood out to you in this chapter and don't forget to include the link to your identity on your **Who I Am in Christ** *page.*

God fights for ME
Exodus 14:13-14

*ponder * pray * journal*

Week Six

Worship is Warfare

"You must remember when waging war with the forces of hell, endurance is the name of the game!"
- Rick Renner, Living in the Combat Zone (1989) [The Complete Guide to Christian Quotations, Perseverance #13, pg. 340]

[Note: This chapter contains two parts. You may want to take two weeks to complete this chapter; one for each part, in order to receive the full benefit of the lessons.]

Part One: Stand

War. It's a topic known to all. We don't like it. We don't like to talk about it. Yet there have been wars since the beginning of time. Throughout history the people of God have been in one battle after another. Some they have won. Some they have lost. If we were to look back through the Bible at the times God told His people to go to war against their enemies we would see what caused success or failure.

> *We battle, but with one difference: we win. It's a fixed fight.*

It's no different today. We battle spiritually every day, every minute of every day. That may be difficult to believe yet it's true. We battle, but with one difference: we win. The tables have been turned. The deck is stacked. It's a fixed fight.

Now that we have our armor on, the time has come to go to war. Don't let that scare you, brave warriors. We are more than conquerors. We saw with our own eyes that overwhelming victory is ours. Overwhelming? You better believe it, sisters!

How do we gain overwhelming victory? What must we do? It's come down to the wire. There's no more time to prepare. The clock has struck the hour and the battle is at hand. It's time to face the enemy.

When you step into church, what is the first activity (after announcements of course)? Worship. But let me be clear. Though music and singing in church is called worship (and it *is* worship), there are other acts of worship we do in the church setting. For instance, our giving of tithes and offerings is a form of worship. Prayer is a form of worship. Uplifted hands are a form of worship. Though worship can be construed as a technical term, for this portion of the study, I want to show you what worship is regarding battle. Read on!

Worship is the battle cry. Worship is the action that, however it is presented, gets the attention of the Father. He is listening. He is waiting. Waiting for what? For you to give Him the open door to fight your battle. You simply need to take your place and stand firm.

There is someone else listening too, dear Warrior Princesses. The enemy is also listening. He hears, too. He's watching. He's also angry because he knows he is already defeated. He couldn't scare you. He couldn't intimidate you. He couldn't confuse you because you made the decision to put your focus on the Lord and worship Him. Worship, sisters, worship the Lord before you go into battle because...

Worship is warfare.

When you begin to sing, to worship God, amazing things start happening. God responds to your sincere, heartfelt, sometimes fearful, worship. He has done it for our ancestors who went before us and He will continue to be there for us, now, today. He promised.

Read Deuteronomy 31:8 from the NLT below, then answer the questions.

"Do not be afraid or discouraged, for the LORD will personally go ahead of you. He will be with you; he will neither fail you nor abandon you."

Write the first four words on the lines below.

_____ _____ _____ _____

There it is again. God telling us not to be afraid. He also doesn't want us to be discouraged. That can be tough sometimes, especially when our situation appears to be hopeless.

We may think God isn't there, but what does the next phrase say? _____

_____

God promises three things after stating He will go ahead of us. Write those promises on the lines below.

He will _____

He will not _____

He will not _____

In the previous verse lies a hint of a link to your identity. You are *not alone*. God has promised never to leave you, fail you, or abandon you. Therefore, you are never alone. We can talk about it all day, but the fact remains that even when we feel as if we are alone, we really aren't. So, take courage in that today! That would be an awesome reason to worship Him, don't you think? There were others who thought it best to worship God with singing, too. Let's continue our journey.

In 2 Chronicles, we find the armies of the Moabites, Ammonites, and some of the Meunites declared war on Jehoshaphat (pronounced *YeHOshafat*). While that would make anyone terrified, as it did Jehoshaphat, something great was about to happen.

Read 2 Chronicles 20:1-23 (I used NLT) then answer the questions below.

What was the first thing Jehoshaphat did upon being told war was being declared on him?

_____

After begging the LORD for guidance, Jehoshaphat then issued an order to the people. What was it and who did it encompass?

_____

Fasting is important when seeking guidance from the Lord. But then Jehoshaphat begins to pray. *Write on the line below the first thing he did when he started praying in front of all the people of the community.*

_____

I met a very special woman several years ago who had a wonderful testimony. She had been given a very disturbing and hopeless diagnosis from her doctor. She was told she had cancer and was not given very many months to live.

The doctors had run some tests then sent her home to await the results. She went home to be with her family and to enjoy what time she had left. While she was waiting, she received a couple of visitors one day; a woman and her little girl. The youngster was also battling cancer.

As they talked, the little girl looked at the woman and said, "Don't you believe in God?"

"Yes, I do."

"Then why are you acting like you're going to die?"

This profound, yet truthful statement from an innocent, but brave, child was just what the woman needed.

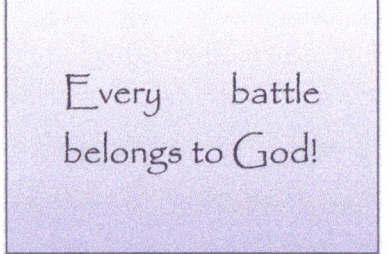

When her visitors left, the woman went to her favorite comfy chair, grabbed her Bible and said, "Thank you Lord, for healing me." She then began looking up every Scripture that talked about healing.

The next doctor visit the woman had, the doctors were stumped. The test results all came back negative. There was absolutely nothing wrong with this woman! However, she wasn't stumped at all. She knew her God had gone before her and fought her battle for her. All she had to do was worship Him.

In our passage we just read, Jehoshaphat began to honor God, to worship Him by telling Him how great He is and reminding Him of all He had brought His people through and all His promises to the people. After that, Jehoshaphat said one more thing.

What was the last thing he said to the Lord?

_____

When you don't know what to do, look to God for help. We really should seek His guidance first in all things. Even though sometimes we are suddenly presented with a problem, like the woman I mentioned above, and we are so taken aback by it we just don't know what to do.

However, check out what it says in Matthew 6:33 below, from the New Century Version (NCV).

"Seek first God's kingdom and what God wants. Then all your other needs will be met as well."

When we look to God first, above all other things, what does it say will happen?

_____

All our other needs will be met. Don't you find that comforting, dear sisters? I certainly do. If we put God first, the things God wants us to do, He will meet our needs.

In **2 Chronicles 20**, I find it awesome and amazing that after the people have all fasted, the king has prayed, asking for the Lord's guidance, telling him they don't know what to do, God sends a message through one of the men standing with all the people, wives, little ones (meaning babies), and children.

Notice, in verse fourteen, the Spirit of the Lord came upon one of the men. Not the king, one of the *men* in the community. This shows that God works through *any* of His people, not just a choice few. Which means, dear Warrior Princess, He will work through you, too.

Go back to 2 Chronicles 20:15 and write the first thing he said the LORD said to the people. "_____

_____ _____ _____!"

There it is again. God telling His people not to be afraid. In my Bible there is an exclamation mark after that sentence. Apparently, God thought it greatly important this time that these people know they should not be afraid. He meant what He said.

Let's break down the next statement in that verse. In the first part of that verse, what were the people told next?

_____

God didn't want the people of Judah to be discouraged by the mighty army. There were three armies preparing to go to war on Jehoshaphat and his people. I don't know about you, but I might just be feeling a little intimidated; okay, a whole lot intimidated. However, God is a good, good Father and He knows what's best for His children. If He tells us not to be afraid and not to be discouraged, then we should do our best to listen to Him.

Look at the next phrase in that statement. What does it say? Write it below.

_____

It makes more sense when we discover that the battle we are about to face isn't even ours to begin with. The battle belongs to God. *Every* battle belongs to God! But here's where it gets even better. God, through His Holy Spirit, revealed to the people not only how the enemies were going to come against them, but also how they were to fight.

They were given prior knowledge. It's like when we play hide-and-seek with our children. When one grownup hides, the other reveals the hiding place to the child so he can win. Well, God isn't hiding, but He sent the Holy Spirit to reveal the enemy plot to the people so they would know what to do to win.

In verse 17, what was the first thing the people were told about the upcoming battle?

_____

What were the instructions after that? There were three steps they were to take.

Step One: _____

Step Two: _____

Step Three: _____

Again, the people were encouraged to not be afraid, not be discouraged, and twice it is mentioned that the Lord would be with them.

Right after receiving this Divine message, what did Jehoshaphat and the people begin to do?

_____

Even before the enemy armies showed up, the people began to worship God. But the next morning is when things got real.

On the way to the battlefield the king stops and begins talking to the people. After he encourages them, he begins sending people out.

Who did King Jehoshaphat send first and what was their duty?

_____

_____

This is where the war begins. Singers, who went out ahead of the army and began singing praises to the LORD. Remember earlier in the chapter when we discussed various forms of worship? Looking at this part of Scripture, we can clearly see that in this time, before a great battle, it was in fact the singing that began the battle. Therefore, we come to the fact that indeed, *worship is warfare*.

Look again at the passage. When the people began singing, what immediately began happening? (v. 22)

_____

_____

The LORD doesn't kid around when it comes to the battle. We often get ourselves in a tizzy worrying about how we're going to handle things when we don't even have to handle it in the first place. The battle is not ours. It belongs to God and He is more than capable of taking care of things and us. He never loses.

When we have on our full armor and are prayed up, then begin our battle by worshiping God, He finishes the fight even before it begins. This is what we have been leading up to. Not only did the armies of Ammon, Moab, and Mount Seir start fighting amongst themselves, they killed each other. The army of Judah didn't have to do a thing…just like God said.

It's no different for us. When we stand, just as we were told to do, we will still be standing when the battle is over. Sound familiar?

God doesn't stop there, even.

Read 2 Chronicles 20:24 (I used NLT). What did the army of Judah find when they arrived at the lookout point?

_____

What did they find when they went to gather the plunder? _____

_____

They didn't have to fight. They were to worship the LORD first, then stand still and watch God fight for them, and after it was all over with they even got rewarded? Yes! They were given the possessions of the enemy. All of it!

Oh, lovely Warrior Princess, do you not see that even today your fight is fixed? You win! Just like the people with Jehoshaphat were given victory over their enemies, so have you.

You may be wondering if this even applies to our lives today. It does. We may not come against huge armies as the people of Judah did, but we still have war declared on us emotionally, mentally, and spiritually. Sometimes it even gets physical and that often changes the battle plan. We have discussed that periodically throughout this study. Yet, God never meant for us to live in a state of fear, but to stand, boldly, praising Him and let Him fight our battles no matter how small or insignificant we think they may be. If it's important to you, it's important to God because you are His child and He adores you.

Debriefing:

In this part of our study we have learned that it is important to have our armor on at all times. We discussed not only that it's time to stand and fight, but also that we will have overwhelming victory. We don't have to be afraid because the fight is fixed, but also that every battle belongs to God. However, one of the most important things about this section is that worship is warfare, and there are many types of worship.

You can journal this portion on the journal page at the end of this chapter.

Worship is Warfare

Part Two: There's a Time to Run

Every good soldier knows when to stand and when to run. When the troops deploy, they have times when they stay still. They don't move. Yet they are in battle. However, when the C.O. (Commanding Officer) gives the order, the troops advance. They run forward, at the enemy, fully armored, fully prepared, straight into battle.

While we've studied being bold and standing firm against our enemy, knowing all we need to do is stand still and let God fight our battles, there comes a time when we do need to run. However, that doesn't mean we run in retreat. The time will come when we must run *at* the enemy. Toward. Sword raised. Shield up. Battle cry on our lips.

Run at the enemy.

Let's face it, we live in hostile times. We always have. This world is not our home. Yet, we are placed here for a time and purpose known only to God. He has a reason and purpose for having you and me in this time period. We were chosen for here and now. *We* are the ones who are capable, through Him, of handling the battles before us.

Yes, we will have times when we do stand and watch the LORD fight for us. Other times He will tell us to run at the enemy. It will be during that time when God makes a show that will impact many and may just change your life in the process. But how will we know whether to stand or to run? By having faith in the Lord and asking Him for guidance, then doing what the Holy Spirit tells us to do.

In 1 Samuel 17, we see the Philistines have gathered their army for battle against Israel. Yet another battle looms with God's people and their enemy. As Saul gathered the Israelite troops on one hill, the Philistine troops gathered on the other hill with the valley in between (1 Samuel 17:1-3).

There is quite a difference in this scenario than from the one we read about in 2 Chronicles. In 1 Samuel 16, Samuel had been instructed by God to anoint David to become the next king of Israel. David then found favor with Saul, the current king, and was serving the king as his armor bearer while still also tending his father's sheep.

It was during this time when the Philistines had come against Israel. The enemy stands on a hill, ready to strike the people and they don't know what to do. They are being intimidated by the enemy; mocked, ridiculed, laughed at. Little do they know things are about to change for everyone, including David.

Read 1 Samuel 17 then answer the questions below (I used NLT).

As the Israelites and Philistines are in a stand-off, who is it that takes the initial step forward?

_____

How does the Bible describe Goliath and his armor? _____

_____

_____

_____

I don't know about you, but if a man who was over nine feet tall stepped out from the ranks of the enemy's army, I think I might be *more* than a little bit intimidated! It wasn't bad enough that this giant of a man steps out from the ranks of the troops, he then begins taunting the Israelites.

Read 1 Samuel 17:8-10 again. What kind of taunts did Goliath yell at the Israelites?

_____

_____

_____

When Saul and the Israelites heard these things, how did it affect them? _____

_____

How many days did Goliath taunt the Israelites (v. 16)? _____

Dear Warrior Princesses, these are the very same things you and I come against every day. While they may not sound exactly like what Goliath said to Saul and the Israelites, they are threats, taunts, and intimidation nonetheless. And just like our ancestors before us, we often react the very same way, terrified and deeply shaken.

Can you imagine being taunted by the enemy for forty days? Some people have been taunted and terrified by the enemy (the devil) longer than that. Not everyone knows they are under enemy attack. They believe they were either born that way, inherited their condition, or some even believe they actually did something to cause themselves to be in the situation they are in. Some people believe that God is punishing them and they deserve to be miserable. Not true.

Oh, but lovely ones, things are about to change.

Read James 4:7-8a below from the NLT, then answer the questions.

> *"So humble yourselves before God. Resist the devil, and he will flee from you. Come close to God, and God will come close to you."*

What is the first thing we need to do? _____

Who are we to resist? _____

When we resist the devil, what will he do then? _____

In verse 8 it says to come close to God. What will God do? _____

_____

God is always waiting for us. He won't invade our lives, because He is a gentleman. Yet, He loves us too much to leave us alone. While the Israelites are cowering before their enemy, someone comes along and decides enough is enough.

David begins asking the members of the Israelite army not only what the reward would be for killing their enemy, but I believe he was beginning to feel righteous anger. Not self-righteous anger, but righteous anger. There's a difference.

David became angry because the Philistine was defying whom (last part of verse 26)? Write his exact words from that verse on the lines below.

_____

_____

David wanted to know just who did Goliath think he was, coming against the armies of the living God? Apparently the Israelite army had forgotten who they were, too. But read that last part again.

"Who is this pagan Philistine anyway, that he is allowed to defy the armies of the living God?"

If you look at the end of that sentence, you will discover another link to your identity. Not only were the Israelites God's people, so are we. Therefore, as His daughters, His Warrior Princesses, we are *part of the armies of the living God* as well.

Maybe you don't feel like you're part of an army. But if you've come this far in this study, my dear ones, you can bank on this fact. Not only are you all those words you've been writing on that page in the back of the book, you are also one of God's troops. You are a *warrior*! Write that one down in all capital letters on that special identity page and be proud of it because as a WARRIOR you are also *undefeated*.

Let's move on...

David has begun asking questions, looking for information regarding the demise of this enemy who is taunting the armies of the living God. The armies have forgotten who they are. They have forgotten their identity. Even Saul has fallen victim to the taunts and believes they are already defeated.

Although the Israelites believe there is no hope, what does David say to them (v. 32)?

_____

David is doing something that the Israelites should have been doing all along. He's putting his faith in God for victory. He's standing firm in his faith. He's believing God. He's walking boldly and confidently, declaring out of his mouth that he will fight the Philistine and win (vs. 34-37).

David has declared he will fight the Philistine (Goliath), but how does Saul handle it?

_____

Whenever we step out in faith to do what the Lord has called us to do, there will be those who rise up to prevent us from moving forward as we've been called. They will try to change us, give us their advice, discourage us and often times stand in our way to prevent us from completing the task we know we're supposed to accomplish.

Look at verses 38-39. What did Saul give to David and how did David react? _____

_____

We can't wear someone else's physical armor any more than we can be like someone else. We can try, but it's never a right fit. We are all made to be unique. Therefore, we should all be ourselves and operate in the gifts God has given each of us specifically. I can't walk your walk and you can't walk mine. But we can come alongside one another and spur each other on, encourage one another, and help each other when we need help.

Read Deuteronomy 14:2 from the NKJV below.

"For you are a holy people to the LORD your God, and the LORD has chosen you to be a people for Himself, a special treasure above all the peoples who are on the face of the earth."

Wow! Would you like to talk about who you are now? There are so many links to your identity in this one verse. We have already discovered we are chosen. But look at all those identity markers. Warrior Princesses, you are a ***holy people*** to God. You are chosen to be someone just for Him. Think about this for a minute. It says the LORD chose you to be a people for Himself. You have been ***handpicked***. That's another link, precious one. It doesn't stop there though. It goes on to say that you are also a ***special treasure***. How humbling is this to know God personally handpicked each one of us to be a special treasure to Himself? I can hardly contain it. Oh, don't stop there. Immediately after we discover we are a special treasure, it says we are *"above all the peoples who are on the face of the earth."* Did you catch that? We are ***above***, not beneath. Hard to take it all in? I understand.

Read Deuteronomy 28:13 below from the NKJV.

"And the LORD will make you the head and not the tail; you shall be above only, and not beneath, if you heed the commandments of the LORD your God, which I command you today, and are careful to observe them."

In this astounding verse you find more links to your identity. Not only does it confirm that you are **above and not beneath**, you are also **the head and not the tail.** This simply means that if we follow what God has told us to do or not to do, we will be in front, not behind. He will elevate us. He will prosper us. He will more than take care of us if we simply follow Him.

Looking back at David, now we can see how important it was to him that someone stand up to the Philistine enemy who was making snide remarks about God. David was about to do what the Israelite armies wouldn't, or maybe couldn't.

As David prepares to go to battle with Goliath, he not only took off Saul's armor, which didn't fit, he only chose five smooth stones from a stream and put those in his bag. As he walked out across the valley, they only thing he was armed with was his shepherd's staff and his sling (v. 40).

Now, as with any big bully, of course Goliath is going to continue to taunt, even curse David. David replies to Goliath's taunts.

On the line below, write the last sentence in verse 47 (I used NLT).

_____

Goliath had been defying God and his people for forty days. As David started across the valley to face off with his enemy, the last thing he said to the Philistine was the promise God had given to the people long ago.

"This is the LORD's battle, and He will give you to us!"

Look at verse 48. The enemy advances. What does David do? _____

_____

David ran at the enemy.

There *is* a time to run; a time to run at your enemy. Though we discussed in Part One of this chapter the importance of standing still and watching God fight our battles, there comes a time when we must run at our enemy. This is the time to engage him in battle. Remember, though, you have already won. Therefore, show him. Stand up against him. You have that authority. Also remember, God goes before you and He is your rear guard. So run, dear lovely ones.

Run at depression.
Run at anxiety.
Run at bi-polar.
Run at cancer.
Run at all disease.
Run at all oppression.
Run.
Run, Warrior Princess.
RUN!
Draw your sword and run!

You are promised overwhelming victory. You are promised you will be more than a conqueror. Do you know what it means to be more than a conqueror?

David defeated Goliath that day. He not only knocked him down with a sling and one stone, he killed that over nine-foot-tall giant with his own sword and cut off his head. Can I get an "Amen!" Not just that, but here is where David became more than a conqueror; he killed Goliath, cut off his head to prove he had defeated this Philistine who had come against the living God, and David also kept all of Goliath's armor. He was rewarded for conquering the enemy. That is what being more than a conqueror is, precious ones. We not only win, we receive the rewards.

Once David killed Goliath and the Philistines saw it, they turned and ran. This gave the Israelites enough courage to finally take a stand and run at their enemies as well…and they won.

When we take a stand against our enemy, when we declare God openly with our mouths and trust Him for victory, we will be victorious. Not only that, but our enemies will turn and run when they see our victory.

> There's no need to fear any battle.

There's no need to fear *any* battle. There will be no casualties. However, you must understand, if we do nothing, if we never give God the glory, never worship Him, if we never stand, if we never run at the enemy, the battle will never be fought and we will remain captives in whatever is holding us down. We, as

Warrior Princesses, must stand. We must take our place in God's army. We must fight the battle, which means either standing firm on God's promise of overwhelming victory and watching Him fight our battle for us while we sing His praises, or running at the enemy and allowing God to fight through us to win the battle.

Whatever the battle plan, we win because, remember, the fight is fixed. We are guaranteed victory. We just need to make up our mind to accept that victory on behalf of our good, good Father.

Debriefing:

We have discovered many links to our identity in this chapter. We learned that worship is warfare. Singing praises to God begins the battle. We do not battle alone. We have learned that sometimes we stand and watch God fight for us, but sometimes it is necessary to run at our enemy. Possibly the most important thing we've learned is that the battle is not ours but the Lord's. Our fight is also fixed because we win. We win because God wins and He never loses.

If something stood out to you in this chapter, write it on your journal page at the end of this section. Also, be sure to write all the links you found in both sections of this chapter on the **Who I Am in Christ** *page.*

This means WAR

*ponder * pray * reflect*

Week Seven

Arise, Warrior Princess!

"The great need of the present hour is Christians who have learned to sing the song of deliverance on the testing side of trouble."

-David Wilkerson, "Right Song, Wrong Side" sermon (2009)

We have talked about so much throughout the last few weeks. It can be a bit overwhelming, if not intimidating, when discovering who we really are and who we were meant to be. One thing is certain: God definitely has great big plans for you and me, dear sisters. He has always had good plans for us because He is our good, good Father. What parents don't want the best for their children?

However, knowing God is always there for us, we must remember we can't just sit idly by and expect Him to do everything for us. It doesn't work that way. We have to get up, arise, and take our place as we were designed to do. We must be obedient to the call we have on our lives.

Still not sure of your identity? Not sure you are cut out to be a warrior, much less a princess? Maybe it hasn't sunk in just yet. That's okay. Sometimes it takes a bit for the truth to sink in. Sometimes we need confirmation after confirmation after confirmation. There were several people in the Bible who also needed confirmation, affirmation, realization, and many other "*tions*."

One particular person comes to mind. In the book of Judges, a man named Gideon discovered much about himself, and God, in a short amount of time.

Read Judges 6:11-12 below from **The Message.**

"One day the angel of GOD came and sat down under the oak in the Ophrah that belonged to Joash the Abiezrite, whose son Gideon was threshing wheat in the winepress, out of sight of the Midianites.

The angel of GOD appeared to him and said, 'GOD is with you, O mighty warrior!'"

> We must be obedient to the call we have on our lives.

Here we have dear Gideon, hiding from the Midianites and threshing wheat in the winepress so maybe his people can get a little grain and not have it stolen out from under them like they've had done the last few years (see Judges 6:1-10). While he's hiding, hidden from the enemy, the angel of GOD just appears to him? Absolutely!

How did the angel address Gideon and what did Gideon call him? _____

_____

Now read verse 13 below.

"Gideon replied, "With me, my master? If GOD is with us, why has all this happened to us? Where are all the miracle-wonders our parents and grandparents told us about, telling us, 'Didn't GOD deliver us from Egypt?' The fact is, GOD has nothing to do with us – he has turned us over to Midian."

How did Gideon respond? _____

_____

I'm not sure, but if an angel appeared to me while I was hiding from my enemies and called me a mighty warrior, I don't think I would believe him either. But isn't this how most of us respond to something God says to us?

Yet, even though Gideon was hesitant to believe his identity, he wasn't at all afraid to ask why all this stuff was happening to them when he thought his people were supposed to have been delivered.

Read Judges 6:14 (The Message) below and answer the questions.

"But GOD faced him directly: "Go in this strength that is yours. Save Israel from Midian. Haven't I just sent you?"

Who does it say faced Gideon? _____

What were the instructions He gave him? _____

_____

Who sent Gideon? _____

For just a moment, I want you to look back at the passage you just read. Notice how GOD is written in all capital letters? In the NKJV the word is LORD. Again, all caps. The reference to GOD is the same as LORD. Remember in the beginning of this study, I referenced the different spellings of the Lord's name and their meaning? When written in all caps, regardless of GOD or LORD, this is the Hebrew YHWH, emphasizing His position as covenant maker and keeper.

We are about to see something amazing, Warrior Princesses!

The LORD addressed Gideon by his identity as HE saw him; "O mighty warrior!" He sees you as you are in Christ. Do you not yet see yourself that way? My dearest sisters in Christ, here is possibly the most powerful link to your identity; *mighty warrior*. This is why I chose *The Message* version for this particular section. I wanted you to see, in print, exactly how God saw Gideon, but also how he sees *you*. As a warrior. Though the verbiage in other translations is different, the meaning is the same. We are warriors, plain and simple.

There are times, however, when even I don't feel mighty, much less a warrior. Forget it. Lord, I'm not mighty, nor a warrior so please don't put them together and call me a mighty warrior! Yet, that's exactly who I am! That's who you are! Believe it, because it's true.

Yes, we are currently reading about Gideon. However, this could very well be your story, dear sister. It sure used to be mine. Maybe you're hiding out, trying your best not to be seen by anyone, enemy or otherwise. You just want to quietly exist, no attention brought your way; don't anyone notice me, address me, or ask me to be part of anything. Especially don't ask me about my situation or things I've been through or done. I would be mortified. Is that you?

I've been there. Depressed, intimidated, embarrassed, fearful, or worse, I open my mouth and say all the wrong things and embarrass myself further. Yes, dear sisters, I've been there.

But that is not who I was, nor is it who I am today.

Neither is it who *you* are. We have come so very far in this study in discovering our identity in Christ; who we are in Him, who He says we are. Now is the time to arise, Warrior Princess. Now is the time to take your place in God's mighty army, because you have been called, appointed, chosen, anointed, gifted, and challenged. You have a mighty call on your life to rescue those who are where you once were.

God can heal us of anything, even depression, anxiety, intimidation, and poor self-image from verbal and emotional abuse. My call is to help rescue and encourage those who are suffering in the same things. Your call may be similar or it may be different.

Maybe you are recovering from alcohol or substance abuse. Rescue those who are where you once were.

Maybe you were once a victim of sexual abuse. Rescue those who are where you once were.

Maybe you were once addicted to pornography. Rescue those who are where you once were.

Maybe you were once a victim of domestic violence. Rescue those who are where you once were.

Maybe you were once addicted to gambling. Rescue those who are where you once were.

The list is endless, my friends. Whatever you are going through, there is someone or several someone's who are going through the same things you once struggled with. Your call is to help rescue them out of it and show them the Love of Jesus. You may be the only Jesus they see because no one else will hold their hand out to them to lift them out of the pit they are in.

You know, when the LORD (all capital letters) addressed Gideon as "mighty warrior," Gideon wasn't quite sure how to take that. He asked the Lord about it. This is where I find such encouragement. Whenever the Lord gives us instructions, if we don't understand, we absolutely *can* ask Him questions and He will help us understand. In other words, it is okay to ask "why?" provided we don't question His authority. Simply ask for wisdom in understanding what He just told you.

Read Judges 6:15-16 below from the NKJV.

"So he said to Him, "O my Lord, how can I save Israel? Indeed my clan is the weakest in Manasseh, and I am the least in my father's house."

"And the LORD said to him, "Surely I will be with you, and you shall defeat the Midianites as one man."

Gideon was a bit confused as to how he was supposed to save an entire nation (Israel), from such a huge army of enemies. His clan was small, he (Gideon) was small, and he just couldn't wrap his mind around what he was being told. So he asked questions.

What did the Lord tell Gideon? _____

_____

Maybe you're a bit confused about your role, your calling. I admit, it can be a little intimidating, especially when you've never done anything like that before, or even if you never thought you would or could be of much use to the Lord. However, if the Lord says He will be with you, you can believe what He says. He never lies and He always comes through on His Word.

Let's look a little deeper at that conversation. Watch the spelling. Gideon addresses Him as Lord. However, when He answers back to Gideon, the Bible addresses Him as LORD (all caps).

This is intentional. Gideon acknowledges the Lord in His position as Master. Even though he isn't certain at this point exactly Who he is conversing with, he still has the presence of mind to know he is in the presence of someone in a position of authority over him, someone holy. Therefore, he addresses Him as Lord; lower case letters, emphasizing lordship and position as Master.

When the LORD answers Gideon, He was already announcing the covenant with him and that He was Gideon's keeper, meaning no harm would come to Gideon or his people.

I find this exceptionally profound and a bit exciting. How many people did not know this would be written in God's Word one day? Yet here it is for you and me to know and to learn and ponder the magnitude of how far God will go to rescue His people, but also to let us know exactly Who He is to us at that moment.

It's also understandable to be slightly confused about *how* He will do what He says. Nevertheless, Gideon still asks and the Lord, ever so patient, answers him.

Read Judges 6:17-22 (I used **The Message***).*

Even though the Lord had said He would be with Gideon and that he would defeat the Midianites as though he were one man, what did Gideon ask the Lord? (vs. 17-18)

_____

Isn't that just like us today? God gives us instructions, encouragement, and we ask for a sign to be sure it's true.

What did the LORD say to Gideon, though? _____

God is so patient, loving and kind! He *waited*. In Gideon's day, it was proper to bring an offering to the Lord, as Gideon did. **Then something miraculous happened. What was it?**

_____

In the words of a famous comedian, *"Here's your sign!"* What more could a person want? Here Gideon brings unleavened bread, meat, and broth as his offering to the Lord. He places the bread and meat on the rock and is told to pour the broth over the offering. Now it's wet, but as the angel of the LORD stretches out the tip of the stick and touches the bread and meat, fire breaks out of the rock and burns up the bread and meat! Gideon now knew *Who* he had seen and been talking to and comes completely undone. I think that would have me shaking in my mismatched socks, too.

While Gideon is having his moment, the Lord speaks to him again.

Read Judges 6:23 below from **The Message.**

"But GOD reassured him, "Easy now. Don't panic. You won't die."

I love how *The Message* Bible puts things in such down-to-earth verbiage. The first thing the LORD does is tell Gideon to calm down, then He reassures him that he won't die. "You're not going to die. I just told you you're a mighty warrior and are going to defeat this huge army as if you were one man."

Why would God take him out of the equation when He just told him he was about to do something amazing? Let's look at it another way; Why would God take *you* out of the equation when He just told you you're about to do something amazing? Yet, isn't this exactly how we think today? We automatically begin thinking negatively, preparing for the worst even though we have a great calling on our lives.

My dear warrior sisters, this is a ploy of the enemy, to whisper lies into our minds and get us to snowball them out of proportion so bad we cause ourselves to panic. When we overreact to the enemy's lies, we put the brakes on the Lord's plans. We inadvertently slow our own progress because of fear, uncertainty, panic, indecisiveness, and just blatant disobedience.

Yet, even when we realize what we've done, the enemy loves to instill fear in us that the Lord is mad at us and going to *zap* us into oblivion. He instills in us false fears to prevent us from coming boldly to God and allowing Him to bring us back into a right relationship with Him. That's how we find so many today who truly believe God can't use them anymore, if ever. We find our sisters (and even brothers) in Christ in a proverbial fetal position spiritually, unable to move, much less utter the words needed to engage the Holy Spirit for help. They have allowed the lies of the enemy to stop them in their tracks and cause them to believe their lives are over.

But God's Word says otherwise.

Look at Psalm 118:17 from the NKJV below.

"I shall not die, but live, And declare the works of the LORD."

Just as the angel of GOD spoke to Gideon and told him he would not die, what does the first part of the above verse assure us?

_____

Instead, what will we do? _____

_____

Again, if God has saved you, called you, anointed you, appointed you, and chosen you (remember writing all these links?) do you really think He is going to allow you to die before you walk out your assignment?

You shall not die, but live!

It's very easy to become confused about what might happen when God gives you an assignment. Let's remember that the enemy wants us to be confused. He wants us to fail. Therefore, he will plant obstacles in our way to prevent us from being victorious.

Read Judges 6:24-32 (I used NKJV).

The LORD gave Gideon an assignment and he carried it out. But then what happened?
Write your answer on the lines below.

_____

_____

_____

_____

There will always be someone or something that stands in your way. However, when you are obedient to what the LORD tells you to do, great things will begin to happen.

In Judges 3:33-40, though the people were angry with Gideon for destroying their idols, God blessed Gideon. The Spirit of the LORD came upon Gideon and when he blew the trumpet, people came from all around to gather. Remember, there was an army against them. These people had been living in fear, being bullied and enslaved by their enemies the Midianites.

The Israelites were in slavery once again because of their disobedience to God. For seven years they were in bondage. However, when they cried out to the LORD, He heard them and God raised up a deliverer to bring them out of bondage once again. This is where we find our story.

The Spirit of the LORD (the Holy Spirit) had come upon Gideon and now he was gathering the troops, preparing to take on the enemy. But God begins to thin out the numbers.

In Judges chapter seven, God thins the Israelite troops from 22,000 men down to a mere 300 to defeat the Midianites. Why was this so important?

Read Judges 7:2 below, from the NKJV.

"And the LORD said to Gideon, "The people who are with you are too many for Me to give the Midianites into their hands, lest Israel claim glory for itself against Me, saying, 'My own hand has saved me.'"

On the lines below, write the reason the LORD told Gideon there were too many people for Him (God) to give the Midianites over to the Israelites.

_____

_____

When God gives an assignment, He will provide the way and means for you to be successful. If we look back on the last chapter, we recall we either stand and watch the LORD fight *for* us, or we run at the enemy and allow Him to defeat said enemy *through* us. Remember, our fight is fixed. We win. No matter what. All we have to do is be obedient to our calling.

> When God gives an assignment, He will provide the way and means for you to be successful.

Gideon was obedient and lived. His people lived. Their enemy? They died. How? Just as the LORD told Gideon they would. Now remember, a lot of things happened in between, but I want to focus on the actual event. Gideon was in fact obedient to what the LORD told him to do. In doing so, victory was won.

Yet, even in our victory, the victory is not ours but belongs to God. The fight isn't even ours. The fight belongs to God. Therefore, if we take credit for the victory, even though we were the ones who conquered, we are doing God a great disservice. It's not about us, lovely ones. It's all about God.

I know it must sound like a *catch-22* statement, but it's not. We are all part of God's historic and amazing plan. We have no idea the magnitude of our role in His work. We just need to remember that His ways are much higher than ours. His thoughts are much greater than we can imagine. But one day we will know and when we do what a glorious revelation we will behold!

In our study, we saw a warrior rise up. My dear, sweet sisters in Christ, you are also a warrior. It is time that you as well rise up. You will be victorious. You will conquer. You will overcome, because this is who you are. This is what you were born to do. You are living in the time you are meant to live in. You were designed to do the things you do in this life. And you are promised victory.

Make no mistake, though, if you do nothing the battle will not be won. People will not be set free. You will not advance in your spiritual walk. You will never win the victory if you don't arise, Warrior Princess!

You cannot advance if you are continually living in the past, continually waiting for the Lord to move. He *is* moving. He is always moving. But He is waiting on you. Dear lovely ones, I have watched, in sadness, listening to women talk about knowing they have a call on their lives yet sit, waiting, watching to see what the Lord is going to do. One of the most frustrating statements I've heard repeatedly is, "I can't wait to see what the Lord is going to do!"

Lovelies, He is doing stuff *right now*. God is a right now God. He has given the instructions. He is waiting for his Warrior Princesses to arise *now*. God has sent the Holy Spirit to guide us, to lead us, to teach us, and to deliver us. The Holy Spirit is so much more than we allow Him to be simply because we won't move.

Stop waiting. Start moving. Don't let the enemy keep you idle one minute longer.

Below, read Isaiah 51:4-8 from **The Message.**

"Pay attention, my people. Listen to me, nations. Revelation flows from me. My decisions light up the world. My deliverance arrives on the run, my salvation right on time. I'll bring justice to the people. Even faraway islands will look to me and take hope in my saving power. Look up at the skies, ponder the earth under your feet. The skies will fade out like smoke, the earth will wear out like work pants, and the people will die off like flies. But my salvation will last forever, my setting-things-right will never be obsolete.

Listen now, you who know right from wrong, you who hold my teaching inside you:

Pay no attention to insults, and when mocked don't let it get you down. Those insults and mockeries are moth-eaten, from brains that are termite-ridden, But my setting-things-right lasts, my salvation goes on and on and on."

What does He say comes from Him? _____

Therefore, if we want to know anything, we must seek the LORD, our Covenant Maker, our Keeper. He never breaks His covenant with His people. He is always right on time.

When does He say His deliverance and salvation come?

Deliverance: _____

Salvation: _____

Looking at Gideon, remember that, after he tore down the idols, what happened the next morning? He had people come against him. We will have that as well, but God has something to say about those who mock us and insult us.

From the last paragraph in the passage above, write what God's Word says, on the lines below.

_____

_____

Sometimes it's easier said than done when it comes to not letting the words of others get us down. We have to remember who we are and Whose we are and then we can stand with confidence, knowing that His deliverance and salvation will come right on time, as always.

Let's not stop there, lovely warriors. ***Look up and read Isaiah 51:12-23 (I used NKJV for this passage) and answer the questions below.***

Even in our fear sometimes, we forget the LORD.

In verse 12, how does He encourage us even then? _____

_____

Looking down at verse 14, what does it say about the one held captive? _____

_____

The captive wants to be set free. Those who are in bondage to one thing or another don't want to be there. Those who suffer depression never planned on having it. Those who are addicted to alcohol or drugs didn't plan to get in that situation. The one who sneaks into the night to view pornography didn't plan to do those things. The one who feels enslaved in a physically abusive relationship never planned for that to happen.

None of the people in these situations ever planned to be where they are. Yet, they are. Many of them don't know how to get free from their captivity. They may be fearful for not only themselves but for others who may be involved. This is how the enemy adds chain link after chain link to the bondage we suffer. We see no way out, so not only are we held bound by the chains of our infirmity, regardless of what it is, we also feel hopeless that we will ever see freedom from our situation.

But God has other plans; not only for them but for you. You, dear sister warriors, have the answer that someone somewhere needs. How do I know? ***Read Isaiah 51:16 from the NKJV, below.***

"And I have put My words in your mouth; I have covered you with the shadow of My hand, That I may plant the heavens, Lay the foundations of the earth, And say to Zion, 'You are My people.'"

Look at the first sentence in that passage. What does the LORD say He has done?

_____

You don't have to worry about what to say, lovelies. He has already put the right words in your mouth; *His* words. All you have to do is be willing to stand up and speak. But that isn't all He has done for you and me.

Fill in the blank below from verse 16 above.

"I have _____ you with the _____ _____

_____ _____."

Wow! Being covered with the shadow of His hand, do you not realize that you are being protected? We have just uncovered another link to our identity, dear ones. We are *covered* (protected) by His hand. His personal hand. The LORD personally covers us. Isn't that enough to spur you on, give you encouragement, excite you into moving forward, or make you throw your hands in the air in praise to Him?

He has explained in the last part of verse sixteen the reason He put His words in our mouth and covered us in the shadow of His hand.

On the lines below, write the LORD's promise.

That I may _____,

_____,

*And say to Zion, "*_____.*"*

What encouragement! Look at that last statement. There is another link to your identity. You, dear one, are *His people*. You can literally claim, *"I am God's people."* You are HIS.

Having said that, if we look at the rest of the passage, we will find even more ways He sets the captives free. Though we are attacked by the enemy, the LORD is going to turn the tables on those who oppress us.

Look back at Isaiah 51:21-23 (emphasis mine). The LORD has something to say to you.

> *"Therefore please hear this, you afflicted, And drunk but not with wine.*
> *Thus says* <u>*your Lord, the LORD and your God*</u>*, Who pleads the cause of His people: 'See, I have taken out of your hand The cup of trembling, The dregs of the cup of My fury; You shall no longer drink it.*
> *But I will put it into the hand of those who afflict you, Who have said to you, "Lie down, that we may walk over you." And you have laid your body like the ground, And as the street, for those who walk over.'"*

There is a very important message within this passage. The LORD wants to make it clear to you and me the seriousness of what He is about to do. I have emphasized it purposely so you would notice.

There are many people who simply cannot wrap their minds around the fact that God doesn't want to harm them, but free them. They cannot understand that He loves them unconditionally. They can't understand, much less believe, that He has great plans for them and that they are somebody in and for the kingdom of God.

Maybe rather than looking at who *we* are, we need to look closer at Who *HE* is. We need to look a bit closer at that in this passage. So let's break it down as He has given us all three descriptions (as we noted at the beginning of this study) in this one verse alone! I have written them all out individually with their descriptions below then we will break them down separately.

In the passage above, it you will notice, *"Thus says your Lord."*

Lord. The Hebrew transliteration is a form of *Adonai*, emphasizing God's lordship and His position as Master.

Next in the same sentence is, *"The LORD…"*

LORD (in all caps). The Hebrew *YHWH* (Yahweh) emphasizes His position as covenant maker and keeper.

Finishing the sentence is, *"and your God."*

God. When you see references to *God*, the Hebrew *Elohim* emphasizes His position as universal Creator.

I find this exceptionally profound, yet oh, so simple, that He addresses those who are oppressed, those who are going through a rough time, those who feel put down, beat down, held captive, dealing with depression, oppression, addiction, or anything and everything that prevents them from having a relationship with a loving God who is crazy about them. That includes you and me.

First, He speaks as Lord. *Your Lord*. He's yours. He's mine. Our Lord, Adonai, the One who is above all. He is Lord of all. Master. Our Master.

> "For the LORD will go before you, And the God of Israel will be your rear guard."
> ~Isaiah 52:12b
> (NKJV)

Second, He speaks as the LORD. Our *LORD*. Our Covenant maker and keeper. The One who never goes back on His word.

Third. He speaks as our *God*. Elohim. Our universal Creator.

He is the First, Middle, and Last, surrounding everything and everyone. He even pleads our case, He prays for each and every one of us. No matter what we have been through, Jesus intercedes on our behalf to the Father. He is our High Priest.

Do you see how we cannot fail? Do you see now how the fight is fixed? We win, dear Warrior Princesses! I don't mind saying it over and over again.

Therefore, there is no reason we cannot arise and be victorious.

Read Isaiah 52:3 from the NKJV below.

"For thus says the LORD:
"You have sold yourselves for nothing, And you shall be redeemed without money."

There is yet another link to your identity. You are *redeemed*.
On the line below, write what position the LORD is in as He has said this.

LORD: _____

We aren't finished yet. Being the Warrior Princesses of the LORD (covenant maker and keeper), there is another, wonderful way He sees us.

Read Isaiah 52:7 from the NKJV below.
"How beautiful upon the mountains Are the feet of him who brings good news, Who proclaims peace, Who brings glad tidings of good things, Who proclaims salvation, Who says to Zion, "'Your God reigns!'"

Do you see another link to your identity in there? You are *beautiful*. Beautiful! He doesn't stop there, though. *Read for yourself verses 8-10 and be encouraged.*

Before we end this exciting chapter you must know, dear Warrior Princess sisters, God adores you. He has set in motion a great series of events all designed to elevate you, to higher standing in your lives, your jobs, the things you seek to accomplish. He wants to prosper you, give you more of what you long for. He wants to enlighten you, to teach you, give you wisdom in the decisions you make. And He wants to give you increase, not only in finances, but health, family situations, and more. The list is endless of all the possibilities He has for *your* benefit. Therefore, everything we do should glorify Him or bring glory *to* Him.

Yes, the enemy means to harm us. He will do everything he can to mess us up. He wants to see us defeated. But what he means for harm, God will turn it for good if we follow His plan and are obedient to the call set upon our lives.

We have been appointed as watchmen for our brothers and sisters in Christ, to help them realize who they are and help rescue them and free them from bondage. Only when we realize that we belong to God, take our stand, and voice our position will we be successful.

One last thing I want you to see before we close is that we never have to worry about fighting for the LORD.

Read Isaiah 52:12 below from the NKJV.

*"For you shall not go out with haste. Nor by flight;
For the LORD will go before you, And the God of Israel will be your rear guard."*

Where do we find the LORD? _____

Where do we find God? _____

Oh, lovely Warrior Princesses, our Yahweh, our Covenant Maker and Keeper, goes before us as we go out to battle, and our God, our Elohim, our universal Creator, is our rear guard! He leads us and He watches our back!

I am literally in tears as I write this. I cannot fathom the magnitude of it all, yet I am as excited as I can possibly be as I let all this sink in. Not only are we God's special people, we are His anointed, appointed Warriors. His royal children.

We cannot be defeated because He is never defeated. We always win because He does. All we have to do is be who He says we are.

So… Who are *you*?

Debriefing:

In this exciting chapter, we have discovered it's time to arise as God's Warrior Princesses. Just as Gideon, named a warrior, arose to God's call into battle to save his people, so we must take our place to do likewise. Not only have we discovered more about our identity in Christ, we have also discovered more about who God is as our Lord, Master, Covenant Maker and Keeper, and universal Creator. Knowing this about Him helps us realize that we are never alone and no matter what the enemy throws our way, as long as we know who we are and do what God has called us to do, we will be victorious as well as helping to free others from their oppression.

Use your journal page to write down anything that jumped out at you in this chapter. Also, don't forget to write the links to your identity on your Who I Am in Christ page in the back of the book.

O, Mighty Warrior!

*ponder * pray * journal*

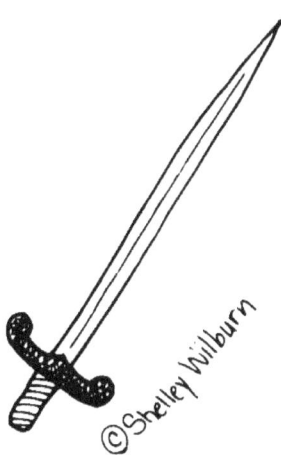

Week Eight

Live Free, Live Brave

"Freedom is not just freedom from restraint; freedom is freedom to do what God has empowered you to do." -Mel Lawrenz, Jubilee *(2008)*

My dear, Warrior Princesses, we have come so very far in our journey of discovering who we are in Christ. Every link we have written down is just a piece in the puzzle of our life's journey. Every link is exactly who God says you are, yet these identifying words are not even one drop in the bucket of eternity to explaining your true identity.

I would encourage you to continue digging through God's Love Letter to you (the Bible) and continue writing down all the beautiful things He says about you. While you're at it, remember that you are free to live as God intended for you to live.

As a Warrior Princess, you have the freedom to not only live free but live brave. Stand, dear ones. Take your place among the saints who have gone before you. You haven't earned it. You haven't bought it. But it was bought for you by the blood of Jesus Christ, Himself and given to all those who ask for it. It is a gift of freedom like none other; one that lasts an eternity.

The enemy will squawk, balk, and cause trouble. Let him. When you know who you are and Whose you are, he cannot touch you. When you put on all your armor and take your stand, using the authority Christ gave you, the enemy can only slink away in defeat. He *is* defeated. He will remain defeated. There is nothing he can do that will turn the tables in his favor. Remember that.

In this chapter we are going to add a little more to our identity. This chapter is dedicated to freedom and bravery, so let's find out what God says about that.

Read John 8:36 from the NLT below.

"So if the Son sets you free, you are truly free."

Who has set us free? _____

If the Son, Jesus, has set us free, then we are free. That means from everything that has the potential to defeat us: death, hell, addiction, depression, anxiety, abuse, our mistakes, everything. We no longer live in that subdued attitude. We are truly, really, unequivocally free. In that verse is another link to our identity. We are *free*.

Why then, do we continue to bring up the past mistakes of not only ourselves, but others? Human nature is often blamed. Many people attribute our words and actions to happenstance. I do not. I suspect a vicious, conniving enemy who slinks and prowls, stalking us, waiting for a chance to whisper those lies into our minds then watch for us to let them grow into a slippery slope to cause us to slide back into old habits, thoughts, and emotions.

Don't let him do that to you. Don't let anyone do that to you.

We have the very power to turn things around, raise our sword (God's Word) and be overwhelmingly victorious. We have the power to live free and live brave.

In John 8, there is a very powerful statement.

Look at John 8:32 from the NLT, below.

"And you will know the truth, and the truth will set you free."

Can you write what truth this is talking about? _____

_____

Jesus is our Truth and knowing Him sets us free. But also knowing His Word will *keep* us free. It's a very profound discovery when you think about it. The more we read the Word, the closer we get to the Lord. The closer we get to the Lord, the more He reveals to us.

Throughout history, the people of God have been enslaved and freed numerous times. In the Old Testament when the people of God would slide back into sin, old habits, or do what they thought was right instead of what God told them was His plan for them, they would find themselves back in slavery. Many times, God would give them over to their enemies to be held captive for however long it took for them to realize they had done wrong. Sometimes the people would even just sell themselves into slavery thinking it would make things easier on them. It never did.

Don't misunderstand God's actions, however. Though He is loving, fair, just, and righteous, God also does not allow sin. God is perfect. He cannot sin and He cannot lie. He hates those things, but He never hates us. God gives us many opportunities to make a U-turn. He is the God of second, third, fourth, and many more chances. But His patience does run out, especially when His children continue on a downward path, living in sinful ways, doing sinful things and never returning to Him. Often times, He will send someone who can get through to us and help us to see where we strayed. Yet, it is always up to us whether to return to God or continue on our own way.

God freed His people whenever they have cried out to Him. It may have taken a long time in some instances, but God is always on time. He is always working, always setting things up in our favor. Remember from the previous chapter, the fight is fixed – we win. *Always*.

In every passage, we have discussed setting people free because they are enslaved to something. Our enemy, the devil, would like nothing more than to keep us held captive by one means or another. But Jesus came so we could be free, be healed, and live an abundant life. Because of our freedom, we are no longer slaves to the sin that holds us prisoner.

Look at 1 Corinthians 7:22 from the NLT below, then answer the questions following.

"And remember, if you were a slave when the Lord called you, you are now free in the Lord. And if you were free when the Lord called you, you are now a slave of Christ."

On the line below, write your *definition of the word* slave.

_____

What does it mean to you to be free in the Lord? _____

_____

Were you a slave when the Lord called you? Think about that for a minute. Was there something that held you captive, preventing you from having a complete relationship with Jesus? Was it depression, anxiety, addiction, abuse, or an illness? Was it worry, un-forgiveness, unbelief, holding a grudge, or something else? What were you doing when you finally felt the Lord tugging on your heart? When you finally turned to Him and asked Him to be your Lord and Savior, He set you free in Him. All those things mentioned above no longer have a stronghold over you.

* * *

I must pause right here in our study for one minute. If you have come this far and are still having difficulty identifying with the links to who God says you are, if you are still struggling to come to grips with that, may I ask you a question? Do you truly know Jesus as your Lord and Savior? I don't want you to miss an opportunity to come to know Jesus for the first time, if you have never made Him Lord of your life.

Therefore, I have added an appendix in the back of this book to help you. If you will turn to that page and read through it, I want to give you the opportunity to enter into the most wonderful, loving, rewarding relationship you will ever have. Then come back and finish the study. We'll wait.

* * *

Dictionary.com defines slave as *"a person who is the property of and wholly subject to another; a bondservant."* We can become slaves to many things and even people. But the point of the matter is, whatever you were going through before you came to know the Lord, even before you were freed from whatever troubled you and held you captive, you were a slave to that. All those are things that hold us captive and prevent us from living that abundant life Jesus died to give us.

However, when we come in contact with Jesus, we can never be the same. He changes us. He frees us. Look at the last part of the verse above. To be called by the Lord is great. Once we surrender ourselves to Him we step into that glorious walk. It doesn't mean our lives will be without trials or events that challenge us. We will have many challenges and battles along the way. But our attitude going into it will determine the outcome. Will we be positive and brave, or allow the negativity to consume us?

Being a slave of Christ doesn't mean we are in bondage again. We are still free. A slave of Christ only means we have become sold out to Him and have risen up and declared our allegiance to Him, our obedience to Him, and will do whatever He has called us to do.

Once we realize we are truly free in Christ, we should be bold in our walk. We should begin walking in the anointing He has poured out on us and run in the calling we have on our lives. Maybe that sounds farfetched, but in truth it is more real than you can possibly know.

However, there are some who never begin to live in the freedom Christ died to give us. Instead, they use their freedom to do whatever they choose to do, blatantly disregarding God's instructions. They make excuses for why they are doing the things they do and living the way they are. These are very dangerous waters, my friends.

Read 1 Peter 2:6 from the English Standard Version (ESV) below.

"Live as people who are free, not using your freedom as a cover-up for evil, but living as servants of God."

How are we supposed to live? _____

In what way are we to live (to use our freedom)? _____

_____

Again, being a servant of God, a slave of Christ, only means that we have become so in love with Him that we can't do anything but what He has told us to do. It's not foolish. It's not ridiculous. However, to those who are not living for Him, it is. In fact, it is repulsive.

Look at 2 Corinthians 2:14-17 below from the NLT.

"But thank God! He has made us his captives and continues to lead us along in Christ's triumphal procession. Now he uses us to spread the knowledge of Christ everywhere, like a sweet perfume.

Our lives are a Christ-like fragrance rising up to God. But this fragrance is perceived differently by those who are being saved and by those who are perishing.

To those who are perishing, we are a dreadful smell of death and doom. But to those who are being saved, we are a life-giving perfume. And who is adequate for such a task as this?

You see, we are not like the many hucksters who preach for personal profit. We preach the word of God with sincerity and with Christ's authority, knowing that God is watching us."

Below, you will find the two types of people mentioned in the above passage. *Write how each one perceives the fragrance of those whose lives are Christ-like, then tell how their perception affects you.*

Those who are being saved: _____

_____

Those who are perishing: _____

_____

My thoughts regarding both: _____

_____

_____

Don't forget, Warrior Princesses, we are in a battle every day. We come in contact with people who are in bondage of one sort or another. Some know it, some do not. Many are looking for a way out and don't know where to turn. Others do not know it and therefore are put off by someone such as yourself who has decided to allow God to heal them and then walk in that healing. You, dear sisters, who have discovered who you are in Christ and have taken the stand to become God's Warrior Princess, can be a help to some but a threat to others.

Your walk will be a threat to someone, or several someone's out there who are not living in the grace and mercy of a loving heavenly Father. Instead, they will become negative toward you. These are the ones God may just place in your path. Although, if you remember who you are and Whose you are, you will be victorious. You won't always be able to rescue everyone who crosses your path, and sadly, some people just don't to be rescued. It doesn't mean we failed. By stepping out in faith to do what God has called us to do, we remain victorious.

Remember to stand your ground. Stand for Who you believe in. You never have to be ashamed to stand for Jesus. Instead, you can live free and live brave. Never move or be moved from your faith in Christ.

As we have studied throughout this book, God made a covenant (in the Old Testament) with our ancestors who have gone before us. He is our covenant maker and keeper. He keeps His covenant and never breaks it. In other words, He never goes back on His word and never breaks a promise. In the passage above, we have living proof from the New Testament, through Jesus, that the covenant was fulfilled and a New Covenant put in its place.

You may be asking what that new covenant is. If you'll look back at the passages, you will see. God is leading us along *"in Christ's triumphal procession"* and He uses us *"to spread the knowledge of Christ everywhere, like a sweet perfume."*

Those who know Christ will smell that sweetness on us. Those who do not know Christ, or who are not living for Him, will not smell it. Instead, we will put them off.

I know that may sound redundant to some, but as we walk along in our journey, we must remember this so as not to get discouraged and also not think ourselves more highly than we should.

Look at Colossians 3:24 from the NLT below.

"Remember that the Lord will give you an inheritance as your reward, and that the Master you are serving is Christ."

It's easy to get sidetracked. However, when we remember Who we serve, the magnitude of our journey becomes even greater.

On the line below, write the identity of the One you serve.

_____

It is a great honor to serve the Lord, to minister to others who suffer in things we have been healed from. It is a great honor and exciting to discover who we are in Christ and then share it with those who haven't realized who they are. Together, we form one powerful force that even the gates of hell can't break.

Therefore, what difference does it make whether we rescue others or not? What is the cause of our journey? It certainly includes our own rescue, our own discovery of who we are in Christ. However, it is much more than that.

Every day our faith is put to the test. Every day we find another obstacle from the enemy, a wall he tries to erect to keep us from ministering to those in need. Whether or not they realize they're in need of a Savior, many people are being bound in the chains of abuse, neglect, depression, anxiety, addiction, sold into slavery, human trafficking, and much more. Even our very minds are being attacked by those who would promote their own agenda doing what's *"right in their own eyes"* (Isaiah 5:21).

The enemy (the devil) does not want you or anyone else to discover your true identity. If you do, you become an even bigger threat to him and his plan to destroy what God put into motion. The devil hates God. Because he cannot be part of God's magnificent plan, to live in the beautiful eternity of heaven, he has been doing everything he can since the beginning to ruin eternity for God's people. Us.

Yet, the one thing we've studied over and over throughout this book is that he *is* defeated. He can't win... unless you allow him to. Remember, the only power the devil has is the power you give to him. Therefore, if you speak negatively either about others or yourself, you are giving the devil a foothold into theirs and your destruction.

So, how do we prevent ourselves and others from sinking back into old habits, abuse and addictions?

Read Galatians 5:1 from the NASB.

"It was for freedom that Christ set us free; therefore keep standing firm and do not be subject again to a yoke of slavery."

Who set us free and for what? _____

Now that we are free, what do we do? _____

_____

*What are **not** to do?* _____

_____

Do you know what a yoke is? Merriam-Webster's Dictionary defines yoke as; "Something that causes people to be treated cruelly and unfairly especially by taking away their freedom."

If we stand firm in our faith in Jesus, we prevent ourselves from becoming slaves again to those old things that once held us down and prevented us from living in the freedom Christ died to give us.

It's a journey. It's a battle. It's a process. However, it's not too difficult. If it was, we wouldn't be able to do it. With Christ's help, of course, we can.

Be aware though, you will encounter people who will proclaim that it's just too hard to do. They have been tricked into believing that they can never get well, can never overcome illness, never get out of that abusive relationship, never get over addiction, depression, never get past their past, or never be able to forgive, or be forgiven. They have been conditioned to believe they are nothing and mean nothing. These are the ones who are being lied to, quite often, by the very people they love the most. I understand. I have been there, too.

Still, we have a job to do, a mission. We are called to a great ministry, dear ones. But don't just take my word for it, take the word of the apostle Paul: *"I, therefore, the prisoner of the Lord, beseech you to walk worthy of the calling with which you were called, with all lowliness and gentleness, with longsuffering, bearing with one another in love, endeavoring to keep the unity of the Spirit in the bond of peace"* (Ephesians 4:1-3, NKJV).

You and I are much more than we know. We can do this. It's not too difficult because we have Jesus on our side, walking with us through every minute of every day of our lives, even in the midst of trials. We can be brave. God has given us such great gifts to use in our journey.

Read Ephesians 3:11b-12, from the NKJV below.

*"...in Christ Jesus our Lord,
in whom we have boldness and access with confidence through faith in Him."*

God not only gave us Jesus as our Lord, but He also gave us a few other things through Him. ***On the lines below, write what they are.***

_____

> You and I are much more than we know.

Not only are these things gifts, but they are also links to our identity. You, dear Warrior Princesses, are **bold**, **confident**, have ***faith***, and ***have access to the Father***.

It's not just about living brave, living free, and having the confidence in Christ to walk our walk and walk in our anointing. We can run in our calling with the freedom knowing nothing, not even the devil, can stand in our way.

Knowing who we are in Christ, knowing who He says we are, we are free to worship and serve Him in ways that are deeper, more meaningful, and more abundant than we ever imagined possible. It's so exciting to live in such freedom from those chains that held us captive for so long. How much more exciting to be able to help others realize it, too!

Look up and read Ephesians 3:14-21 (I used NKJV).

The apostle Paul, writing to the church in Ephesus to encourage them, has given them a glimpse into the total love of God. It's sometimes difficult to fathom, even now. However, Paul gives us more than just a glimpse, but we can also find more links to our identity.

In verse 16 we can see how Paul wished that God would grant us strength through His Spirit (the Holy Spirit), that Christ would dwell in our hearts through faith. But reading on, we find links to our identity.

Read Ephesians 3:17-19 from the NKVJ below:

"...that Christ may dwell in your hearts through faith; that you, being rooted and grounded in love, May be able to comprehend with all the saints what is the width and length and depth and height – To know the love of Christ which passes knowledge; that you may be filled with all the fullness of God."

In the passage above, can you find the links to your identity? I'll give you a hint; there are four. Write them below.

_____

_____

_____

_____

How awesome to discover we are **rooted** and **grounded in love**, we have **comprehension**, and we are **filled with the fullness of God**. Maybe you wrote more than that, which is just fine. I hope the Holy Spirit spoke to you and showed you something else to your identity that only He wanted you to know. If so, how exciting!

If we look past the verses above, we find one more link. Look back into Ephesians 3:14-21. In verse 20, you will find one more link to your identity. Through Christ, we have **power**. His power works in us. It works through us. It is not our own, but His. However, it is part of who we are.

Ephesians 3:20-21 is also a doxology—a prayer of praise to God. We should praise Him every day, several times a day. Let's be clear, we don't have to be in church to pray and praise God. Pray and praise in your car, while doing the dishes or laundry, praise Him while exercising, or sitting. Pray and praise with your eyes wide open so you can see the glorious things the Lord wants you to see. Above all, praise Him with expectancy. Expect Him to show up and to answer you. God never tires of hearing us praise Him. We should never tire of praising Him. Because, without Him, where would we be? Certainly not here, discovering who we are in Him.

God has chosen us to be Christ's representatives on earth. What a marvelous position. How humbling to know He loves us, chose us, saves us, heals us, promotes us, and sends us. It's overwhelming to know this much alone, but to consider the magnitude of our calling and what that means is priceless.

Dear Warrior Princess sisters, have you realized who you are? Do you know how far you've come in this journey? Why then, would you even consider going back into your old ways? Why would you pick back up old habits? Why would you ever think you could wear those broken chains again? You can't.

It would be a great disservice to the LORD, our Covenant Maker and Keeper, to retreat. Therefore, stand, dear ones! Stand in your newly found identity. Raise your chin just a little higher, smile that beautiful smile, raise your hands in victory and praise to the One who has saved us, healed us, and made a way for us to be more than victorious.

Hallelujah! He is worthy!

Freedom. Bravery. These are two words which may seem foreign to you, but as you begin your new journey in who you are in Christ, you will begin to realize how powerful they are and how important to your journey.

It is time for us as God's Warrior Princesses to stand, not only in our identity, but our calling. It is time to rise up and take our place in history, for we were not placed here by accident. Oh, no, dear ones, we are right where we are on purpose *for such a time as this*.

This is our time. While the world rages and others march for one thing or another, we know the truth, God's truth, Jesus. We know what we are to do. It's time to stand and do it.

Don't be afraid.

Be free.

Be brave.

Debriefing:

In this chapter we have discussed the importance of living not only free but brave. We have talked about what it means to be slaves to the things that keep us in bondage; however we have also talked about what it means to be a slave of Christ. Jesus freed us so it is very important for us to stay free, live free, and live brave so we can minister to others who are in bondage and help them discover their freedom and who they are in Christ. We are Christ's representatives here on earth, chosen to bring a most loving word to those seeking freedom.

If something stood out to you in this chapter, write it on your journal page at the end of this section. Also, be sure to write all the links you found to your identity on your **Who I Am in Christ** *page.*

Live Brave

ponder * pray * reflect

Who I am in Christ

©Shelley Wilburn

Debriefing

It is your business to restore the integrity and the righteousness in the high places of this land, and let the people see examples which will be helpful to them in their Christian life.
- Henry Drummond, A Life for a Life and Other Addresses (1893)

Discovering your identity in Christ is a lifelong journey. The links in this study are only the beginning. God's Word says so much more about you and to you if you'll but take the time to search.

As I was putting the final touches on this study, the word "links" jumped out at me. I realized that connecting these links to our identity was not only helping us discover who we are, but these links were connecting to form a very strong piece of armor called chain mail. Chain mail is an impenetrable piece of armor, worn like a shirt, to protect your chest, your heart and vital organs, from attack.

Wear yours proudly!

With those links, those descriptive words, comes a calling so profound and magnificent it can bring us to our knees in humility. Like Moses, who are we that God would choose us to bring His Word to others? Yet, He has. He has bestowed such a gift upon us; how can we refuse?

There is an army rising up. This is an army of women, chosen by the Most High God. This army of women has God's favor. They are each called into various areas to bring good news. That good news is you don't have to live in captivity any longer. There is a way out. Jesus provided the way. All you have to do is step into it. He will do the rest.

God is raising up an army of women throughout the world. However, we must know who we are in Him before we can stampede into the masses and be successful. When we figure out who we are then we step into our identity and role as Warrior Princess.

We are royal.

We are more than conquerors.

We are His.

Women have been oppressed for far too long. It is time for God's Warrior Princesses to arise and take their place as not only watchmen, but rescuers. There are many out there already, working, serving, ministering. But they need help.

Once you know who you are in Christ, you become more powerful. You become more aware. You become who God designed you specifically to be. You also become an even bigger threat to the enemy. So wear your armor at all times. Be prepared. Yet, also be brave.

The battle is not ours, but the Lord's. He will fight for us, with us, and through us, if we will be obedient and stand in faith for Him. We may need to stand still to win the battle. We may need to run at the enemy to win the battle, though make no mistake, we will win. The fight is fixed. We will be victorious, but we must make a move. Idleness will win us nothing.

Being a Warrior Princess is more than just about being a warrior. It's about standing up for you—it's about being who you are in Him in such a way that it draws others to you. That's how you rescue your sisters in Christ.

Others will see each of us and be drawn to Christ in us. The Holy Spirit draws people to each of us. When we walk in our anointing, operate in our calling, boldly, with confidence, knowing who we are in Christ that will emit a wonderful fragrance that some people cannot resist. That's when the door is open for you to minister.

Being a Warrior Princess is so much more than just discovering who you are in Christ. We must walk it out every day. We must exercise the gifts He has given us. We must be alert every day to recognize when He has placed someone in our path to encourage, inspire, and rescue.

Some may not know what it is, but they know there's something different about you. You, dear ones, are called to bring healing and hope to your sisters so they can realize they are a Warrior Princess, too.

This is not a competition. It's not a comparison. We each are unique and we should operate in our uniqueness. It would be pretty dull if we were all the same and had the same gifts. Yet the LORD uses many of the same gifts in us but in different ways, which adds volumes to our uniqueness…still, we serve the same Lord. He never changes, although the more we serve Him the more He changes us. How exciting this is!

Jesus gives us the freedom to choose our walk. He gives us freedom to live abundantly our life journey here on earth and one day we will transition into eternity where we will continue to live abundantly forever. How awesome to think while we were here on earth we helped Him to rescue others to live out that abundance.

Wouldn't it be exciting to know someday in eternity that we were the vessel He used to cause a domino effect of people helping rescue people out of the clutches of the enemy? I think so. Until then, we have a wonderfully magnificent calling.

You are a Warrior Princess!

Stand tall, stand strong, keep your armor on and encourage those around you. If I never meet you in person here, I will meet you in eternity and we will celebrate.

Yours in God's Army,

What Do All Those Links Mean?

We have been writing words through this entire study. We have called them links to our identity. But what do all those links mean? Although they each describe who we are in Christ, as I was writing this book, I discovered something powerful. Have you discovered it?

Look back at the Who I Am In Christ page. If you only look at the words, you'll definitely see a plethora of descriptive words, which alone tell an amazing story about the awesome woman who wrote them down. You. I hope your inner warrior has been awakened and the fires ignited afresh. As we stand together, sister warriors, I want to show you one more piece of armor that you may not have noticed was being weaved, link by link, throughout this study.

As we have written down each descriptive word, each link has been forming what is known as chainmail. What *is* chainmail? In medieval times, chainmail, or mail as it was often called, was tiny links of metal which was forged, then woven, or linked, together to form one large piece. It was then sewn onto a shirt as a protection against the blows of a sword, arrow, or other weapon used by the enemy. Think of it as a bullet-proof vest of today. Chainmail was also used to make hoods worn in helmets to protect the head and neck, as well as worn on the arms and legs, hands, and even the feet, all worn under metal armor, all used for protection. Of course, with any armor, it did not protect against an attack but it did lessen the blow when struck.

Now, in regards to the links you wrote on Who I Am In Christ, let's do one more activity. Go back through each word, each *link* written, and circle each word. Let your circles overlap. Notice how the chainmail begins to form. When you embrace those words, those links to your identity, each link begins to intertwine. Just as chainmail becomes stronger when linked together, so do your links, sweet warrior! The next time the enemy comes prowling, scheming, plotting and whispering lies, trying to attack you, discourage you, or make you back down from your God-given calling, you remember that you have your chainmail on under your full armor of God. Straighten your crown, dear lovely one. Remember who you are and Whose you are. Put your foot on the neck of your enemy. Then raise your Sword (your Word of God) and strike true. You are a victorious Warrior Princess!

What Does A Warrior Princess Look Like?

Maybe you're wondering what a Warrior Princess actually looks like. She looks like *you*! In the Kingdom of God, we are all the same while also different. In the picture below, this, my dear sisters, is an army rising up. They are mothers, daughters, sisters, grandmothers, encouragers, prayer warriors, supporters, worshipers, writers, singers, dancers, but most importantly, *Daughters of the Most High God*! Come on in. We will scooch over on the sofa so you can plant yourself in the midst of the group, for you, too are a Warrior Princess!

Many thanks to my daughters and my sisters, my spiritual moms, for coming out to support this project. You all mean the world to me and I love you, dearly.

Rachel	Tina	Melissa
Katie	Lanna	Tammy
Rhiannon	Laurie	Trista
Brenda	Kerri	Shelley
Barb	Monique	

Appendix A

How to Accept Jesus into Your Heart

There have been many "How To's" written on how to be saved; how to ask Jesus into your heart for salvation and eternal life. It can get confusing. I was once there myself and allowed the process to become so difficult I spent years wondering if I had "done it right."

If you are not sure whether you will go to heaven when you die, if you're not sure you know Jesus as your Lord and Savior, please allow me to introduce you to Him. He's a wonderful Friend.

There are a few things you need to know:

Everyone messes up. We all sin. But God provided a way for us to get to Heaven and it's easier than people believe it is.

"But now God has shown us a way to be made right with him without keeping the requirements of the law, as was promised in the writings of Moses and the prophets long ago.

We are made right with God by placing our faith in Jesus Christ. And this is true for everyone who believes, no matter who we are." ~Romans 3:21-22 (NLT)

First, know that you've sinned and cannot get to heaven on your own merit. In other words, you can't work for it or earn it.

"For everyone has sinned; we all fall short of God's glorious standard." ~Romans 3:23 (NLT)

"The Lord isn't really being slow about his promise, as some people think. No, he is being patient for your sake. He does not want anyone to be destroyed, but wants everyone to repent." ~2 Peter 3:9 (NLT)

Second, acknowledge that Jesus died for you, and rose from the dead just like He said He would.

"But God showed his great love for us by sending Christ to die for us while we were still sinners." ~Romans 5:8 (NLT)

"…God would not leave him among the dead or allow his body to rot in the grave.

God raised Jesus from the dead, and we are all witnesses of this." ~Acts 2:32b-32 (NLT)

Third, ask Him to forgive you of your sins and ask Him to come into your heart and be your Lord and Savior.

"For "Everyone who calls on the name of the LORD will be saved." ~Romans 10:13 (NLT)

"So now there is no condemnation for those who belong to Christ Jesus.

And because you belong to him, the power of the life-giving Spirit has freed you from the power of sin that leads to death." ~Romans 8:1-2 (NLT)

"The Spirit of God, who raised Jesus from the dead, lives in you. And just as God raised Christ Jesus from the dead, he will give life to your mortal bodies by this same Spirit living within you." ~Romans 8:11 (NLT)

That's it!

Maybe you aren't sure exactly how to do that. Below is a step-by-step way to accept Jesus. Really, there's no right or wrong way to do it as long as you are sincere and humble when you address Jesus. But know this: He is so very loving, patient, and kind. He knows your heart and when you come to Him humbly, simply asking that He forgive you and save you, *HE DOES!* He promises that.

Now it's your turn. Below is a prayer that you can recite to receive salvation. Or simply, in your own words, ask Jesus to forgive you and save you. Just remember to be sincere and humble. And believe in your heart.

"Jesus, I know I have sinned and messed up. But Your Word says that all who call upon you shall be saved. I'm sorry for the things I've done and ask Your forgiveness. Please save me and come into my heart. Thank you, Lord, for eternal life. In Jesus' name. Amen."

If you sincerely prayed that prayer, then Jesus promises that you are now saved. Your name is written in the Book of Life. You are on your way to heaven. That's it! Welcome to the Family of God!

But don't stop there. Please, tell someone your Good News. Tell your spouse. Tell your family. Tell your pastor at church, and if you don't have a church home, I encourage you to get into a Bible-believing church. Whatever you do, don't keep your salvation to yourself. Get with other believers so you can each encourage each other. Share your faith. It's quite simple, though we often make it more difficult than it really is. Basically, just tell people what Jesus did for you. No one can argue with that.

Glossary of Armor

Crown
    A royal or imperial headdress or cap of sovereignty: *diadem*.

Breastplate
    A piece of metal that covers a person's chest and that was part of the protective clothing (called armor) that soldiers wore in the past.

Belt
    A strip of flexible material worn especially around the waist as an item of clothing or as a means of carrying something.
    A similar article worn as a corset or for protection or safety or as a symbol of distinction.

Helmet
    A covering or enclosing headpiece of ancient or medieval armor.

Shoes (sandals or boots)
    An outer covering for the human foot typically having a thick or stiff sole with an attached heel and an upper part of lighter material (as leather).

Shield
    A large piece of metal, wood, etc., carried by someone (such as a soldier or police officer) for protection.
    Something that defends or protects someone or something.

Sword
    A weapon with a long metal blade that has a sharp point and edge.

Chainmail (mail)
    A kind of protective clothing (called armor) that is made up of many tiny metal rings that are linked together and that was worn by knights and soldiers in the Middle Ages.
    Flexible armor of interlinked metal rings. First use: 1822

Endnotes

Note from the Author
1. Reference to Beth Moore Bible study taken from Stepping UP, a journey through the Psalms of Ascent, ©2007 Beth Moore, Published by LifeWay Press

Introduction

Valley of Dry Bones
2. Come Alive (Dry Bones), ©2016 Lauren Daigle, album How Can It Be (Deluxe Edition), Copyright © 2014 CentricSongs (SESAC) See You At The Pub (SESAC) (adm.at CapitolCMGPublishing.com) / Warner Chappell Music (ASCAP) All rights reserved. Used by permission.
3. Ezekiel 37:1-14, New Living Translation
4. John 20:21, New Living Translation
5. John 20:22, New Living Translation
6. John 10:10, Amplified Bible
7. Hebrews 4:14-15, New Living Translation
8. Hebrews 4:12-13, New Living Translation
9. Psalm 33:13-15, New Living Translation
10. Psalm 32:7-8

Battle Lines
11. Quote from Bernard Law Montgomery, Brainy Quotes, https://www.brainyquote.com/quotes/keywords/battle.html
12. Fall of Lucifer, Isaiah 14:12-15
13. Genesis 3:1, Amplified Bible
14. 1 Corinthians 14:33, New King James Version
15. 2 Timothy 1:7, New King James Version
16. James 4:7-8, Amplified Bible
17. James 4:10, New Living Translation
18. Ephesians 6:17, New Living Translation
19. 2 Corinthians 10:3, New King James Version
20. 2 Corinthians 10:4-6, New King James Version
21. 1 Peter 5:8-9, Amplified Bible
22. 1 Peter 5:7, Amplified Bible
23. Psalm 55:2-3, Amplified Bible
24. 2 Corinthians 10:3, New Living Translation
25. 2 Corinthians 10:7-8, New Living Translation
26. Luke 10:18-20, New King James Version

Basic Training

27. Quote from Donna Partow, The Complete Guide to Christian Quotations, © 2011 by Barbour Publishing, Inc.
28. Romans 12:2, Amplified Bible
29. Psalm 119:11, New Living Translation
30. Matthew 4:1-11, New King James Version
31. 2 Corinthians 1:3-5, New Living Translation
32. Hebrews 4:14-15, New Living Translation
33. Genesis 2:18, New Living Translation
34. Jeremiah 1:5, Amplified Bible
35. Ephesians 1:4, New Living Translation
36. 1 John 4:1-6, The Message
37. Acts 17:28-29, New Living Translation

Your Assignment

38. Quote from Rich Mendola, The Complete Guide to Christian Quotations, © 2011 by Barbour Publishing, Inc.
39. Ezekiel 33:7-9, New Living Translation
40. Jeremiah 1:5-12, New Living Translation
41. Romans 11:29, New Living Translation
42. Isaiah 55:11, New King James Version
43. Mark 6:4, New Living Translation
44. Esther 3:8-13, 4:1-14, New Living Translation
45. Jonah 1:1-2, 3:1-2, Amplified Bible
46. Judges 4:4-24, New King James Version
47. Psalm 91:14, New Living Translation
48. 1 John 5:4-5, New Living Translation
49. Romans 8:37, New Living Translation
50. Romans 8:17, New Living Translation

Prepare for Battle

51. Quote from Stormie Omartian, www.topfamousquotes.com
52. Ephesians 6:10-11, New Living Translation
53. Ephesians 6:12, New Living Translation
54. Ephesians 6:13, New Living Translation
55. Ephesians 6:14-17, New Living Translation
56. Ephesians 6:18, New Living Translation
57. Exodus 14:13-14, Expanded Bible

Worship is Warfare
Part One: Stand

58. Quote from Rick Renner, The Complete Guide to Christian Quotations, © 2011 by Barbour Publishing, Inc.
59. Deuteronomy 31:8, New Living Translation
60. 2 Chronicles 20:1-23, New Living Translation
61. Matthew 6:33, New Century Version
62. 2 Chronicles 20:24, New Living Translation

Part Two: There's a Time to Run
- 63. 1 Samuel 17, New Living Translation
- 64. 1 Samuel 17:8-10, New Living Translation
- 65. James 4:7-8a, New Living Translation
- 66. Deuteronomy 14:2, New King James Version
- 67. Deuteronomy 28:13, New King James Version

Arise, Warrior Princess!
- 68. Quote from David Wilkerson, The Complete Guide to Christian Quotations © 2011 by Barbour Publishing, Inc.
- 69. Judges 6:11-12, The Message
- 70. Judges 6:14, The Message
- 71. Judges 6:15-16, New King James Version
- 72. Judges 6:17-22, The Message
- 73. Judges 6:23, The Message
- 74. Psalm 118:17, New King James Version
- 75. Judges 6:24-32, New King James Version
- 76. Judges 6:33-40, New King James Version
- 77. Judges 7:2, New King James Version
- 78. Isaiah 51:4-8, The Message
- 79. Isaiah 51:12-23, New King James Version
- 80. Isaiah 51:16, New King James Version
- 81. Isaiah 51:21-23, New King James Version
- 82. Isaiah 52:3, New King James Version
- 83. Isaiah 52:7, New King James Version
- 84. Isaiah 52:12, New King James Version

Live Brave, Live Free
- 85. Quote from Mel Lawrenz, The Complete Guide to Christian Quotations, © 2011 by Barbour Publishing, Inc.
- 86. John 8:36, New Living Translation
- 87. John 8:32, Berean Study Bible
- 88. 1 Corinthians 7:22, New Living Translation
- 89. Definition of slave, www.dictionary.com
- 90. 1 Peter 2:6, English Standard Version
- 91. 2 Corinthians 2:14-17, New Living Translation
- 92. Colossians 3:24, New Living Translation
- 93. Galatians 5:1, New American Standard Bible
- 94. Ephesians 4:1-3, New King James Version
- 95. Ephesians 3:11b-12, New King James Version
- 96. Ephesians 3:14-21, New King James Version
- 97. Ephesians 3:17-19, New King James Version

Debriefing
- 98. Quote from Henry Drummond, The Complete Guide to Christian Quotations, ©2011 by Barbour Publishing, Inc.

Other Books by Shelley Wilburn

Walking Healed, A Journey of Forgiveness, Grace, and Hope

Written in diary form, Shelley Wilburn's book, *Walking Healed,* is her journey after being healed of over forty years of mental and emotional issues including depression, anxiety, and intimidation. Using snippets of her healing journey along with biblical truths, Shelley takes the reader on a journey of healing, forgiveness, grace and hope, then leads into finding your purpose.

Written for those who suffer the pain and loneliness of depression and intimidation, Shelley reaches down in the black hole, finds those who are hurting and helps them find their way out.

Walking Healed will help the reader realize that even Christians suffer depression. Shelley Wilburn knows and understands this from her personal experience with depression and intimidation. She also knows the freedom from these issues when God heals you and takes you on a wonderful journey of walking healed. Shelley's story of healing helps others know that even depression is curable and "nothing is impossible with God."

Walking Healed Companion Study

As a companion to Walking Healed, the Walking Healed Companion Bible Study is a five-week journey into discovering healing, forgiveness, grace, hope, and finding your purpose. Designed to be used in conjunction with the *Walking Healed* book, Shelley Wilburn leads you into the depths of the Bible to discover healing for whatever holds you captive. She will then lead you in discovering forgiveness, God's grace, and the hope He gives us. The final week, you will begin to discover how all these attributes converge to help you journey to discover your purpose in life.

Walking Healed and its companion study is designed to help women (and men) break free and live the life God intended for them. A definite must read. Available wherever books are sold.

About the Author

Shelley Wilburn was born and raised in West Frankfort, Illinois. She began writing when she was twelve years old. She has written several articles and devotions for various newspapers, women's magazines and newsletters, and also co-authored devotionals. In addition to writing, Shelley is also an avid reader, book reviewer, blogger, and speaker. Using her love of writing, and wearing mismatched socks, Shelley has developed a unique ministry of encouraging others using biblical truths and stories from her own personal life. Shelley is married to her high school sweetheart D.A. They have three grown, married children and six grandchildren. When not writing, you can find Shelley and D.A. zipping down the road in their newest adventure-maker, a bright orange, Mustang convertible Shelley has laughingly dubbed The Pony.

Shelley loves to hear from her readers.
You can find Shelley at:

Her website: www.shelleywilburn.org
Facebook: www.facebook.com/authorshelleywilburn
Twitter: @Shelley_Wilburn
Pinterest: www.pinterest.com/shelleyawilburn
Instagram: www.instagram.com/shelleywilburn
E-mail her at shelley@shelleywilburn.org